CW00556398

Jowett Javelin and Jupiter

THE COMPLETE STORY

Other titles in the Crowood AutoClassic Series

AC Cobra	Brian Laban
Alfa Romeo Spider	John Tipler
Alfa Romeo Sports Coupés	Graham Robson
Aston Martin DB4, DB5 and DB6	Jonathan Wood
Aston Martin and Lagonda V-Engined Cars	David G Styles
Audi quattro	Laurence Meredith
Austin-Healey 100 and 3000 Series	Graham Robson
BMW 3 Series	James Taylor
BMW 5 Series	James Taylor
BMW 7 Series	Graham Robson
BMW M-Series	Alan Henry
BMW: The Classic Cars of the 1960s and 70s	Laurence Meredith
Citroën 2CV	Matt White
Citroën DS	Jon Pressnell
Datsun Z Series	David G Styles
Ferrari Dino	Anthony Curtis
Ford RS Escorts	Graham Robson
Jaguar E-Type	Jonathan Wood
Jaguar Mk 1 and 2	James Taylor
Jaguar XJ Series	Graham Robson
Jaguar XJ-S	Graham Robson
Jaguar XK Series	Jeremy Boyce
Lamborghini Countach	Peter Dron
Lotus and Caterham Seven: Racers for the Road	John Tipler
Lotus Elan	Mike Taylor
Lotus Elise	John Tipler
Lotus Esprit	Jeremy Walton
MGA	David G Styles
MGB	Brian Laban
MG T-Series	Graham Robson
Mini	James Ruppert
Morris Minor	Ray Newell
Porsche 911	David Vivian
Porsche 924, 928, 944 and 968	David Vivian
Range Rover – The First Generation	James Taylor and Nick Dimbleby
Rolls-Royce Silver Cloud	Graham Robson
Rolls-Royce Silver Shadow	Graham Robson
Rover P5 and P5B	James Taylor
Rover SD1	Karen Pender
Saab 99 and 900	Lance Cole
Sunbeam Alpine and Tiger	Graham Robson
Triumph 2000 and 2.5PI	Graham Robson
Triumph Spitfire and GT6	James Taylor
Triumph TRs	Graham Robson
TVR	John Tipler
VW Beetle	Robert Davies
Volvo 1800	David G Styles

Jowett Javelin and Jupiter

THE COMPLETE STORY

Geoff McAuley and Edmund Nankivell

The Crowood Press

First published in 2003 by
The Crowood Press Ltd
Ramsbury, Marlborough
Wiltshire SN8 2HR

www.crowood.com

British Library Cataloguing-in-Publication Data
A catalogue record for this book is available from the British Library.

ISBN 1 86126 562 X

Dedicated to:
Charles Callcott Reilly
Gerald Marley Palmer
Reginald Korner

Typeset by NBS Publications

Printed and bound in Great Britain by Bookcraft, Midsomer Norton

Contents

Acknowledgements   6

Foreword   7

Introduction   8

1   A Concept is Born   11

2   Development and Early Marketing   21

3   A Journey Through the Javelin   33

4   The Javelin Comes of Age   41

5   The Jupiter a Coachbuilder's Car   49

6   The Fixed-Head Coupé Jupiter   72

7   Le Mans – and Monte Carlo Again   84

8   Engineering Developments   106

9   Life After Palmer   112

10   The Jupiter in the USA   122

11   Crankshafts, Gaskets, Gearboxes   133

12   The Bitter with the Sweet   142

13   Buyer's Guide   154

Afterword   165

Appendix – The Sporting Calendar   166

Index   170

Acknowledgements

Thanks are due to these people for their help, encouragement and time over the years:
Donald Bastow
Malcolm Bergin
Chris Gibson
Maurice Gomm (the Gomm saloon Jupiters)
Charles Grandfield
Phill Green
Cliff Howarth
David Jowitt (origins of the Jowett name)
Michael Koch-Osborne, Ian Priestley (pre-war Jowett history)
Reg Korner
Duncan Laing
Ted Miller, (USA history and other contributions).
George Mitchell
Huntley Perry (USA Jupiters)
Mike Smailes
Noel Stokoe
Peter Tutthill (Davidstow races)
Nikki Wise
Tim Wise
Simon Wood

Many Jowett and Jupiter club members world wide.

The following magazines were found useful in our research:
The Motor
The Autocar
Autosport
Motor Trend
Road and Track
Exhaust Notes (Journal of the FCCA)
Sports Car (Journal of the SCCA)
The Jowetteer

Foreword

Over half a century ago the long-established Jowett Cars Ltd launched what were, in competition terms, their spectacularly successful Javelin and Jupiter production cars. Considered advanced in concept and appearance by the cognoscenti, and much admired, the company that manufactured them was forced to withdraw from the motor car business after no more than a further seven years.

My introduction to the idiosyncratic Jupiter, more than three decades back, was a dazzling drive around the country lanes of Essex, the car's driver skilfully and rapidly conducting me using throttle-steering to literally straighten out the bends of the narrow, winding rural roads. He did find it within himself to part with his car, but many owners can only do so with the greatest of reluctance, such is the effect that Javelins and Jupiters have. One Jupiter was owned for forty-three years by a man whose working life was spent at TVR in Blackpool. He only sold it on the strict understanding that the new owner would never bring it back to his town, as he could not bear to set eyes on his beloved even by chance.

Another recounted that he has owned Javelins without a break since he was sixteen. Many years ago the girl he was courting revealed that her father owned a Javelin, and marriage to her was, of course, irresistible. Today he runs a Jupiter.

Sometimes difficult, usually rewarding perhaps in spite of themselves, these Jowetts, so full of character, do have this tendency to remain in long-term possession, and the company once recognized this with the slogan 'They are left to the next of kin'. The social side is strong, with many long-term friendships made and renewed perhaps at local or annual club functions, be they in the UK, Australia, New Zealand or mainland Europe as they sometimes are.

This book puts the Javelin and Jupiter under the microscope, looks at their successes in the production-car motor sport of their time and the personalities involved, and seeks to explain the company's sudden disappearance from the scene, even though it was in no sense financially bankrupt.

Edmund Nankivell

Introduction

The very first Jowett Javelin was registered for the road on 25 August 1944. Just over ten years later a gleaming red Jupiter, the last Jowett-built car, emerged from the factory and was delivered to its customer. This, then, is the production life of the two models that are the subject of this book. Geographically isolated from Britain's main car-manufacturing centre, Yorkshire ingenuity and determination underpinned the efforts of a small band of designers and engineers whose cars set new standards of style and road-holding, standards that continue to attract an enthusiastic following fifty years on.

The Jowett Motor Manufacturing Company was formed in 1901 in tiny premises in Church Street in Bradford, Yorkshire, England. At first only engines, for both stationary and automotive applications, were designed and built, but in 1906 the prototype Jowett car was completed. As a diversion, the six Scott-Jowett motorcycles were constructed, 'wheels and all', for Alfred Scott in 1908. It is typical of the soundness and practicality of their designs that a Jowett engine which first ran in 1904 was still in use thirty-five years later, powering a compressor.

The Jowett name does not seem to derive from a trade or place name, nor does the oft-claimed Norman French ancestor Henri de Juatt appear to withstand analysis. The name and its several variants – including Jewett (there was a 1920s era American car-maker of this name, and indeed Jewett may be the original pronunciation) – most probably derived, in the ancient past, from a fecund and presumably unmarried lass called Juliana, probably living in the Thornton–Clayton area just to the west of Bradford, Yorkshire. Jowett was a common diminutive of Juliana throughout the thirteenth and fourteenth centuries, and even in 1438 a lady called Jowett Barton is recorded as living in York. What makes Jowett special is that it is unusual for a hereditary surname to derive from a woman's name, and particularly from the diminutive form. In the 1881 census two-thirds of Britain's Jowetts were living in Yorkshire, the majority in the Bradford area; thus Jowett is a very Yorkshire name and strongly associated with Bradford.

The Jowett company's founders, William, Benjamin and Ruth Jowett – the offspring of Wilfred Jowett, a blacksmith and general engineer – grew up in Girlington, Bradford. The two boys had left school at the age of thirteen to work for their father, but by his middle years he had become a cantankerous widower, so the three broke away to form their own company.

In 1907 the brothers bought premises in Grosvenor Road off Manningham Lane, Bradford, and when they opened up on their first day they were surprised to find a young man already there. His name was Pat Cleary and they decided to keep him on – and he was still working for the company forty-five years later in the engine test bay! No one knew his age, but even he retired eventually, in the mid-1950s.

Four dozen complete light cars of 6.4HP RAC rating with the trademark water-cooled, horizontally opposed, two-cylinder side-valve engine were constructed before war work took over in 1916. Although self-taught, the brothers soon demonstrated a natural affinity for mechanical engineering, so much so that they became official advisers to other engineering establishments in the locality during that war.

From 1920, from a new factory at the village of Idle just to the north of Bradford, cars of 7HP

Long Four, a roomy family saloon, was introduced in 1923; shown here is the 1928 model.

Sports model of 1928. This was the production version of the Brooklands record-holder.

RAC rating, and powered by a development of the original flat twin engine, began to be constructed in ever-increasing quantities. These were full-size light cars and not cycle-cars, and were designed to be cheap to buy and run. Therefore together with their reliability and relative longevity, they became better known for their low cost of ownership rather than their luxury or performance.

From the outset, the hill-climbing abilities and dependability of their cars led the company and privateers to enter the very popular reliability trials and hill-climbs of the time, and successes in the London to Holyhead, London to Exeter, and the Scottish Six-Day trials brought the company valuable publicity.

Initially Benjamin and William Jowett, along with works manager Harry Mitchell, drove the factory's entries; later, Horace Grimley took over this duty. Horace, whom we shall meet again, joined in 1921, and after completing his apprenticeship became responsible, amongst other roles, for engine development. One such task was to develop a special car for a record attempt at Brooklands where, on 8 August 1928, the International Class G 12-hour and 200km endurance records were taken from Amilcar. Over the years, however, the increase in power that Grimley developed from the flat twin only just kept pace with the increased weight of the coachwork, as the cars, in line with contemporary trends, became more comfortable and spacious. A typically

Jowett innovation was the dual-purpose body, where a five-door saloon or tourer could carry loads of up to 5cwt (250kg) by removal of the rear seats.

There was always a small but significant number of chassis delivered from the factory, typically about forty or so per year. A few of these were built into lightweight 7HP sports cars by Jacksons of Croydon in 1923–4. An owner described it thus: 'The car weighed next to nothing. You sat on the floor and bumped about a great deal, it did a comfortable 60mph, and got there quickly.' It is a reasonable assumption that most of the rest of these chassis were built locally into bespoke commercial vehicles.

Dual-purpose coachwork that first appeared in 1929 – perhaps a forerunner of the modern hatchback.

Four-cylinder 10HP family saloon of 1936.

By the late 1920s the Jowett brothers realized that their design was in need of updating, so in 1928 they brought in Stephen Poole as chief engineer. He introduced wide-ranging improvements such as four-wheel drum brakes, detachable cylinder heads, and the relocation of the gear-change lever from the driver's right-hand position to the conventional location. Factory shipments increased from a low of 2,029 in 1928 to 3,374 in 1934. Sales were fairly flat through the nineteen-thirties, but the company was able to keep output steady by producing a wide choice of specialized commercial vehicles: in 1936 about 60 per cent of all Jowett vehicles built were commercials.

The horizontal twin engine grew to 8HP, and eventually Poole designed a four-cylinder, horizontally opposed, side-valve engine. This 10HP engine was in fact the only new power unit introduced in the interwar period, save for the experimental vertical in-line four that powered the La Roche model, of which only two were built. One effect of this was to crystallize the association of Jowett with horizontally opposed engines.

The company went public in 1935, and the following year Reg Korner was taken on board as specialist body designer. He was responsible for Jowetts becoming more stylish and less basic in outline, another factor that helped sustain Jowett through that difficult decade. That year also saw the introduction of the original Jupiter, a 10HP saloon that was not, however, produced in any great numbers. By then the company had its own canteen, own dance/jazz band and social club, and a very loyal workforce. Benjamin, though, did not see eye to eye with his elder brother over the company's flotation, and retired; their relationship never recovered from this disagreement and they and their families went their separate ways, not even remaining on speaking terms. Perhaps something more than their father's engineering skills and talent was passed down to them.

New management and new management style came into the firm in time to take advantage of munitions and other war work following the outbreak of hostilities in 1939. This meant that the 1940-model vehicles, quite advanced at least for Jowett, with a new synchromesh gearbox, improved steering and brakes, and aluminium cylinder heads designed by engine specialist Harry Weslake, saw only limited production before war work took over completely. Under the new go-ahead managing director Charles Callcott Reilly, another factory building was erected at the Idle site, the workforce quadrupled to 2,000, and shift work introduced. This was a challenging time for the small design team, who had to turn each order into quality equipment on time and within budget. This they generally managed to do, sometimes contributing design innovations of their own. The two engines remained in production throughout the war, powering War Department motor/generator sets, and it was essentially the 8HP 1938 van that was put back into production in 1946 as the famous and much-loved Bradford. This Bradford van, in its several variants, was sold into over sixty export markets world-wide, and provided the financial underpinning of the Jowett company during the post-war years.

Callcott Reilly had not forgotten the aftermath of the previous conflict, when manufacturers had severe problems in returning to peace-time operations, and in a far-sighted move he took the decision that the company would have a completely new car design ready for when the war was over. Things were set to change, and change dramatically, at the Bradford car maker.

1 A Concept is Born

Long before the Javelin became available the eagle-eyed observer might predict its appearance from the livery of this Jowett van. (JCC)

For those of us who were not there at the time, it is difficult to conceptualize the extraordinary undercurrent of optimism that permeated the British people during the darkest hours of World War II. At a time when the world seemed to be in mad turmoil, how could industrialists have the confidence, optimism and enthusiasm to plan for better days ahead? As bombs and 'doodlebugs' rained down on London, Coventry, Plymouth and other industrial centres, an indomitable spirit shone through. 'When the war ends...' was the much-used phrase: no 'ifs', no 'buts', just 'when'.

This, then, was the atmosphere in which the Jowett board diverted their minds from the successful production of wartime tools and arms, to questions of how the company could succeed after victory in Europe. Jowett's managing director, Charles Callcott (Peter) Reilly, was a man of some vision and energy. He had been appointed director in 1939, and had been a driving force in attracting lucrative wartime contracts, and setting up the machinery and infrastructure that the company needed in order to benefit from this work. Having got all this under way, he then turned his attentions to post-war activities, and toward the end of 1941 advertised for a car designer. A gifted young designer, Gerald Palmer, responded, and was invited to Idle where he met other Jowett executives and was given a full tour of the works. He was impressed with the people, but was not sure that a company with no body-pressing facilities would be able to guarantee long-term survival in the post-war era.

Gerald Palmer Moves to Jowett

Palmer was quite settled at this time with Morris Motors, although the opportunity of being given free rein to design an all-new car was a tempting one. Having decided against the Jowett offer, he was surprised late one afternoon, on answering a knock on the door of his Oxford home, to be confronted by Reilly. Before the evening was spent, Jowett's managing director had persuaded Palmer to change his mind, and with an offer of a £500 per annum salary, left a happy man.

Palmer moved to Bradford in January 1942, his wife Diana and one-year-old daughter Celia joining him a few months later. An upper-floor flat in Bradford was something of a culture shock after their pretty Oxford thatched cottage, but at least Palmer had realized his dream of being in a position to design his all-new car.

It is worth reminding ourselves at this point that, despite benefiting from much creative advertising (particularly from the pen of Gladney Haigh), pre-war Jowetts were quite rudimentary in design. Admittedly the faithful horizontally opposed twin cylinder side-valve engine – a Jowett trademark since 1906 – had been joined by a flat four design in 1935, but the Bradford firm was regarded, perhaps a little unfairly, as a creator of rugged if rather agricultural devices: cheap-to-run transportation for canny northern folk.

There seems to be little evidence that on the day that Reilly placed his recruitment advertisement, the board's intention had been to create a ground-breaking range of vehicles; rather, they seemed more inclined to return to earlier values, with the company positioned to capitalize on the new manufacturing tools that wartime manufacture had provided. The pre-war light commercial van would be facelifted by body man Reg Korner (and subsequently re-named 'Bradford'). As for the cars, 'more of the same' was perhaps wanted. As we are about to see, things turned out a little differently.

Gerald Marley Palmer 1911–99

Gerald Palmer, along with sisters Marjorie and Joan and his brother Ron, was brought up by mother Esther and father Will in Umtali, Southern Rhodesia (now Zimbabwe). Will was district engineer of the Beira, Mashonaland and Rhodesia Railway.

From an early age, Gerald held a great fascination for all things mechanical, whether they were pieces of railroad paraphernalia, or the discarded family Model T Ford that he converted into his childhood interpretation of a 'hot rod'. As a boy, he would eagerly await delivery of the latest copies of *The Autocar*, *The Motor* and *Automobile Engineer*, magazines to which he subscribed.

Despite his father's wishes that he should remain in South Africa, at the age of sixteen Gerald persuaded his parents to let him visit England to further his studies. He joined the Institution of Automobile Engineers (IAE) as a student member, and was recommended by them to approach the lorry makers Scammell in Watford. Scammell offered a five-year apprenticeship that he readily accepted. During his time with Scammell he worked for their chief engineer O. D. North, a man for whom he had unswerving admiration.

Palmer's position grew within the IAE, culminating in his becoming a graduate member, secretary and the chairman of the London Graduates Branch. In this capacity he gave a presentation called 'The Control of the Infinitely Variable Gearbox' – though when later he attempted to patent the subject of his speech, Palmer found that the General Motors Corporation of America had beaten him to it by a just few months. Consolation was found back at Scammell however, where he met and later married Diana from the drawing office!

Part-time work now started on the Deroy sports car, and in 1935 he left Scammell to devote himself full-time to the project. After unsuccessfully trying to interest AC and Aston Martin in the design, the prospect of war stifled his attempts to raise cash for further development, and the project foundered. All was not in vain though, because he secured an interview with Cecil Kimber at MG cars at Abingdon, and drove there in the Deroy so as to demonstrate his genius – he hoped! Kimber was impressed, and introduced Gerald to A.V. Oak at the Morris design department, and in due course he was offered a job in charge of MG work under the auspices of Morris, developing revised suspension for the yet-to-be announced MG YA saloon.

With the onset of war, work was now focused on military requirements and aircraft repair. This was a rather stagnant period for Palmer's fertile mind, so he was delighted to be offered the chance of developing a production version of the 'Oxford Vaporiser', a portable anaesthetic device to be used in conjunction with surgical operations in hazardous environments. Much modified from Professor Robert Mackintosh's prototype, Palmer's redesign was both elegant and successful. Any guilt at being employed in a 'Reserved Occupation' was lessened for Palmer by the knowledge that the device saved many Allied lives in the field. Variations of the Oxford Vaporiser are still in use today.

After a short period working on the stillborn development of an unusual Scotch crank opposed piston engine for the SU Carburettor company's John Morris, Palmer spotted Callcott Reilly's advertisement for a chief designer. What happened next is discussed in the chapter text.

In 1949 Palmer returned to the Nuffield Group to work for the British Motor Corporation (BMC), with responsibility for the design of future MG, Wolseley and Riley models. 'This was a glittering prize and I had no hesitation in accepting it,' Palmer later revealed.

With an office next door to the now famous Alec Issigonis, creator at that time of the successful Morris Minor, the two men generally got on well. In his autobiography *Auto Architect*, Palmer observes (somewhat waspishly), 'We shared an arrogance common to designers, he possessing it more deservingly and openly than me.'

Palmer's brief was to design a new MG, Riley and Wolseley saloon car range using standard BMC mechanical components. The task was to maintain the individuality of the brands within the constraints of common componentry. Out of this work came the MG Magnette ZA, the Wolseley 4/44 (and later the larger 6/90), and the Riley Pathfinder. He even found time to design two possible replacements for the MG 'T' type range, along with a proposed twin overhead cam engine, a supercharged development of which produced over 300bhp and propelled Stirling Moss and Phil Hill to record-breaking speeds in the EX181 record car.

During his early time at Cowley, Gerald took on a spare-time project offered him by George Wansbrough, Jowett's late chairman. It involved the design of a rather utilitarian, robust vehicle for use in developing countries – a sort of poor man's Land Rover. Named the Yeoman, this little truck was cheap to construct, but rugged enough to traverse rough terrain. It was originally powered by a Jowett flat twin engine, and later a Perkins diesel. Sadly for Wansbrough, the project did not reach a marketable conclusion.

As if all this activity was not enough, Palmer found the time to design himself a new house to be built at Iffley, near Oxford. It will come as no surprise to find that the curving staircase at Orchard House was inspired by one seen at Alfa Romeo's head office!

For complex inter-personal reasons beyond the scope of this book, Palmer's time at BMC came to an end, and in 1956 he found himself as assistant chief engineer – passenger cars with Vauxhall Motors in Luton. Here he performed design work on the F and FB type Victors, the HA and HB Viva and the PA and PB Cresta/Velox range. On his first visit to Vauxhall's Milford proving ground, he marvelled at the engineering resources available to General Motors' engineers, and reflected on what might have been, had Jowett possessed just a fraction of these resources.

During his last four years before retirement, Gerald was responsible for safety and quality control, not the most exciting of jobs, but with interesting opportunities of meeting important government people.

In retirement, Palmer was far from idle, developing a special hoist for assisting disabled persons, and busying himself with the restoration of his Bugatti T44 and his Targa Florio-winning Mercedes Benz. He maintained his association with Jowett as president of the Jowett Car Club until his death.

The Deroy

The car Jowett wanted Palmer to design wouldn't be his first however, because in 1937–8 he had already built a 'special' which he christened the Deroy, named after the Mozambique town where his father had owned a tin mine. The car was commissioned by a wealthy sometime Brooklands racing lady, Joan Richmond. Sadly, the benefactress changed her mind, but with financial help from a Cambridge post-graduate, the project was able to continue.

The finished product, although powered by a modest side-valve Talbot engine (made in quantity by Scammel for their small 'Mechanical Horse' tractor unit), displayed some interesting and original design thinking. Of particular note was the suspension, independent at the front, being of a modified Dubonnet type, utilizing a single transverse leaf spring. A variation of a De Dion design was installed at the rear, also independent and utilizing transverse torsion bars. Our story will return to this theme. Such was the ingenuity of the suspension design that it subsequently formed the basis of a paper published by the Institution of Automobile Engineers.

A clever, hinged metal cover was designed to cover the hood when stowed (for the Deroy was an open two-seater), which when raised, formed a rigid support on the underside of the hood fabric.

With war looming, Palmer was unable to secure the financial backing that would be required to start commercial production of his Deroy, so the tiny company that had been formed to market the car was disbanded. Palmer kept the Deroy, however, and later employed the services of Jowett's technical head, Horace Grimley, along with the latter's home-made camping trailer to transport the car from Oxford to Bradford, where it was subsequently fitted with a sleeker body and a Javelin engine. We will hear again of Horace Grimley and his camping trailer, but alas the Deroy disappears from our story at this point.

Early Design Work

On his arrival at Jowett, Palmer quickly became acquainted with Korner's work on the pre-war cars, commercials, and the as yet unchristened Bradford van. Soon, however, his attentions turned to producing a saloon car. In his own words, 'I wanted to design a rugged vehicle in the Jowett tradition, simple and robust, low in cost, and suitable for any terrain, world-wide.' As we have observed, the resultant car turned out to be a rather different animal.

Palmer's design tools were somewhat primitive, comprising a drawing board and rudimentary instruments little more advanced than those to be found in the average schoolboy's geometry set. Neither was he overwhelmed with staff: he had the services of two good draughtsmen, Cliff Howarth and Stanley Watkins, and was able to call on the wisdom of Reg Korner (Korner had an important role to play in the Jupiter's creation, as can be explored in the chapter devoted to that model). Of course, other personnel were from time to time placed at Palmer's disposal, not least the aforementioned Horace Grimley, brilliant and long-serving head of Jowett's technical engineering department. The design office was a small room at the end of the main entrance corridor, 'barely big enough for 't swinging of a cat', as Cliff Howarth observed in retirement.

And so was born the design infrastructure of a car that was to set new standards in its class, gain many sporting achievements in its lifetime and incorporate a cleverness of design that stirred the admiration of Alec Issigonis, and even today impresses those who care about such things.

Palmer's team didn't get everything its own way, and other designs were considered by the Board, in particular one from a Russian émigré at the London Design Research Unit, designer and artist Naum Gabo. Using basic seating and mechanical plans provided by Reilly, Gabo proposed a rather futuristic design, a scale model of which was presented to Jowett's chiefs. The art critic Herbert Read seems to have been involved with the project. It is known that on 12 May 1943 Read wrote to Gabo stating, 'Jowett has accepted our terms in principle: £3,000 over three years for the design, and a further £3,000 if it is accepted.' To Palmer's relief however, Gabo's design was eventually considered to be too difficult to produce.

Also at about this time, Palmer's old boss, O. D. North, had visited the Idle works to discuss the use of the North Lucas radial engine. Roy Fedden also came to talk about his own radial rear-engine design. But finally the dust settled and Palmer was able to relax somewhat, safe in the knowledge that it was to be his own conception that would carry the day.

Springfield Works

The Jowett Springfield Works factory at Five Lane Ends, Idle, Bradford was specially fitted out during 1946–7 to receive the Javelin assembly line; however, Jowett's occupation of the site dates back to 1920 when it was bought as a worked-out stone quarry from Bradford Corporation for the princely sum of £100. As part of the deal, Jowett charged the Corporation for tipping rights on the site, thereby effectively paying nothing in nett terms for its new factory! The original building measured just 100 × 150ft (30 × 45m), though the factory was further extended from that date. Much of it was destroyed in a devastating fire in 1930; nevertheless, rebuilding had been undertaken by the following year, and further major expansion took place in the early forties.

In 1954 the facility was bought by International Harvester. In the mid-1980s the buildings were demolished, and in 1987 a Morrison supermarket opened on the site (a part of the 'Enterprise 5' shopping complex that now covers most of the original factory area). The opening of the supermarket was celebrated with a cavalcade of Jowetts through Bradford City, terminating at the new store. An impressive frieze depicting Jowett workers and products can be seen in the supermarket's foyer, and the firm runs a Bradford van in Morrison's livery for promotional purposes.

Close by, an estate road has been christened 'Javelin Way', and the nearby West Yorkshire police headquarters appropriately bears the name 'Javelin House'.

Near to the site of the demolished Springfield works, the headquarters for the West Yorkshire and Aire Valley Police is the aptly named Javelin House. (Geoff McAuley)

The reader who is familiar with the final product that the Javelin became may be surprised to know that the initial design requirements were so vaguely defined. It should be remembered that, at this stage, Palmer envisaged a utilitarian car, cheap to build and with a selling price of less than £500. It would use simple, flat panels that could be dealt with 'in house' at Idle, and the whole car would weigh less than a ton. His initial drawings allowed for short, stubby front wings that did not encroach into the door structure: in this way, the offside front door panel could be made interchangeable with the rear nearside one, and the front nearside with the rear offside. This would save money and – as was subsequently demonstrated by the construction of a quarter-scale wooden model – was in no way stylistically awkward, as might have been assumed. This elegant idea typifies Palmer's ability for what we might now call 'lateral thinking'.

Rare picture of Palmer's original quarter-scale model. Note the stubby front wings to allow for interchangeable doors. (The Motor)

Full-scale Javelin mock-up, mainly constructed from wood. (JCC)

The Javelin Prototype

The designer was desperate to contain overall weight in the new car. He appreciated all too well the advantages in terms of performance, economy and handling that could be gained from lightness, and finally set himself a target that the overall weight should not exceed 2,000lb (approx. 900kg). Also, he was keen to produce a streamlined shape. Wind-tunnel facilities were not available to Palmer, but in fact they were not necessary for him to appreciate that a teardrop profile would produce impressive wind-cheating advantages.

Today's modelling clays were not readily available, although plasticine was used to a limited degree in shaping models of small detail sections of the new car's body. A quarter-scale model was produced from wood by one of Jowett's skilled carpenters. The result was sufficiently impressive for the directors, who quickly approved the design, and presented Palmer not only with the go-ahead, but also the luxury of a rather larger office!

Some secrecy surrounded the project, however. As early as 1 June 1943 the following item had appeared in small print in the classified advertisements section of the little-known *Newcastle Evening Chronicle*: 'New automobile speed record gained by Jowett's post-war model, which won the Board's approval in less than no time.' Interviews with Jowett personnel in later years failed to cast any light on the meaning of this mysterious announcement.

With his two draughtsmen, Howarth and Watkins, and as mentioned, ably assisted by Korner, Palmer pressed on with development of a prototype. At this stage it seemed that an all-steel body would be out of the question, as steel was difficult to obtain and expensive (supplies were based on export achievement – a chicken-and-egg situation for Jowett) and such a design would need large pressing facilities. Various different materials were investigated, including aluminium, plastics and even wood. A trip was made to examine techniques used in the manufacture of de Havilland's Mosquito fighter-bomber, which was of largely wooden construction. Some

Draughtsman Cliff Howarth with Jowetts on the site of the Springfield Works, now a Morrisons supermarket. This photo was taken in 1992. (Geoff McAuley)

assembly work for the Mosquito was being carried out at the Carr Hill body plant of Briggs Motor Bodies at nearby Doncaster. (Briggs will feature again later in our story.)

A Pressed Steel Shell

Cars of unitary construction (where the body stiffness is derived from the roof, bulkheads and door aperture frames) had started to appear on some of the world's more advanced pre-war cars, and Palmer was keen to use this technique. But doubt over the materials to be used dictated that the initial design should have a chassis frame. Two large box-section rails were therefore employed, welded to strong front and rear bulkheads of considerable complexity and strength. Designed in this way, it would not now matter whether

The wooden mock-up adorned with fake chromework. Jowett's only qualified carpenter, Bill Broadbent, is on the left. (JCC)

rigidity could be found in the roof and door frames, and the body could be constructed from any variety of low-strength materials.

As time passed however, it became clear to all concerned that steel pressings would be greatly preferable, and talks began with Briggs who had already been contracted to supply Jowett with bodies for the forthcoming Bradford van. The financiers Lazard agreed to underwrite the venture, and so, spurred on by this new situation, Palmer and his team now knew they had a completely free hand to finalize design details on the basis of a pressed steel shell.

They immediately set to work shaping the car as we now know it. Palmer was particularly taken with late pre-war American shapes, and was a great admirer of US Briggs's John Tjaarda, whose work had played a significant role in the design of the Lincoln Zephyr. Not surprisingly then, the new Jowett's shape would resemble a mini Lincoln. It was later maintained (an impression probably arising from comments made by *Motor Sport*'s Bill Boddy) that the designer had been influenced by Lancia's Aprilia (coincidentally the Aprilia's engine capacity, at 1,486cc, was the same as that of the production Javelin). In later years, however, Palmer maintained that the Aprilia was

not of direct inspiration, although he had once helped a friend to strip one down ('…to see how it worked'), and greatly admired the Italian car's design. Indeed, Palmer denied having been actively influenced by any car in particular, although he conceded that general influences came from all quarters. He was particularly taken by one of Tjaarda's conceptual rear-engined designs that had been displayed before the war at two Ford Exposition of Progress shows held in Detroit and New York: the side windows on this concept model bore an uncanny resemblance to those that would appear on the Javelin. Other designs to catch Palmer's eye were the pre-war Beetle-shaped Steyr Type 50, and the V8 rear-engined Tatra T87.

As to the alliterative name 'Javelin', no one seems to remember how it was chosen. Perhaps it was a decision of the board, possibly taking advice from Jowett's effervescent publicity manager, John Baldwin – though when asked about this in the late nineties, the designer could not remember. However, we do know that the car had been named by the summer of 1945, well before the first production car turned a wheel.

Many visits were made to the Briggs Riverside plant at Dagenham in order to adapt the design

Hand-made body skeleton of the first Javelin prototype, constructed at Idle. (JCC)

for pressed steel construction. It is interesting to note, however, that few fundamental changes were needed from Palmer's original designs. As can be seen from photographs of the prototypes, the door window frames were made rather thicker, the tail became a little 'stumpier' and the bonnet shape was simplified somewhat.

The aforementioned decision to produce a strong chassis frame ensured that, now the car would be made from steel, body rigidity was going to be doubly great. This pleased Palmer enormously: his experience whilst living in Rhodesia had instilled in him the desire to produce a car capable of covering rough terrain with comfort and reliability. He knew that the resulting strength and accuracy of the suspension mountings, along with good ground clearance but low centre of gravity, would allow his design to fulfil his criteria for a 'world car'.

As if all these attentions to the body design and manufacture weren't enough to keep Palmer occupied, he was also required to design the mechanical components of the car – not least, of course, an engine.

Designing an Engine

In parallel with the continuing body design work, he penned a number of possible engine solutions based on the 'established Jowett tradition' of a horizontally opposed cylinder layout. We have mentioned that Jowett had produced a flat four engine before the war (a side-valve unit of 1,166cc capacity) that had been fitted into the Jason and Jupiter saloons. But Palmer wanted to follow the then increasingly preferred design for overhead valves, thus allowing higher compression ratios and thereby higher specific power.

Initially he tried out a cast-iron one-piece cylinder block with two main bearings (not dissimilar to the pre-war four cylinder unit), but when this proved to be coarse and noisy, he introduced a third main bearing, but this time in a one-piece aluminium block. Again, refinement was unsatisfactory due to flexing of the block. These prototypes had a swept volume of 1,184cc, a capacity chosen partly because the taxation formula for British cars at that time was calculated in relation to the cylinder bore dimension: the smaller the

Sectional representation of 1950 version of the Javelin engine. (JCL Publicity)

bore, the lower the tax. A larger engine of 1,500cc was planned for export markets. The smaller capacity engine proved to be satisfactory, but the 1,500cc version was, again, rather harsh. Palmer's third attempt was to have a far more rigid two-piece sand-cast aluminium block, split vertically along the centre line. Renfrew Foundries of Glasgow had some experience of gravity die-casting (having produced crankcases for the ubiquitous Rolls-Royce Merlin engine during the war), and co-operated with Jowett on designing and mass-producing a version of Palmer's latest incarnation. By this time, the advantages of the

1,500cc unit were considered to outweigh the 1,200cc, and the former capacity was adopted for both home and foreign markets.

Previous prototypes had cast-iron cylinder heads with the sparking plugs screwed in from underneath, but in order to improve access, their positioning was relocated to the top on the final incarnation.

It is worthy of note that the die-cast aluminium solution for the block was another first for a UK manufacturer. Already the forthcoming Javelin was beginning to appear somewhat revolutionary.

2 Development and Early Marketing

A furtive look from the passenger of the first prototype, DKY 396. (JCC)

On 25 August 1944, the first complete Javelin, DKY 396, emerged from Idle. This and six more prototypes were quickly put to work in an intensive testing programme under the watchful eye of Jowett's impressive chief engineer Horace Grimley. Challenging routes were chosen from the factory at Idle around the Yorkshire dales, taking in the small towns and villages of Otley, Pately Bridge, Grassington, Kettlewell, Leyburn and Thirsk. These routes embodied many tortuous country lanes and steep hills, not least of which being the infamous Sutton Bank (a one-in-four (25 per cent) switchback ascent barely wide enough for two cars to pass) and its sister single-track hill known as White Horse Bank.

The cars were hammered day and night in an attempt to break them. Certainly a few faults were identified, such as a weakness in the front suspension wishbones, but by and large they behaved remarkably well – a sure testament to good design and sound manufacture.

Prototype DKY 396 was almost immediately followed by DKY 463 and then DKY 612; this latter car seemed to have spent some of its early life in the Midlands and southern counties. It is thought it might also have been used by some of Ford's people at Dagenham in developing techniques for mass production.

It is known that the designer spent many hours at the wheel of DKY 463, and that it was regularly parked outside his Bradford home. In later years a gentleman recalled hitch-hiking a lift in it near

Photos of the first prototype are rare. This snapshot survives in a family scrapbook.

Rear view of the first prototype shows the unique shape to the boot lid and rear wings; these did not survive into production, however. (JCC)

Shapely curves and contours. We refer to the second prototype, of course! (JCC)

the village of Birstwith, and he remembers the bonnet flying open. More development obviously needed!

Liaison continued with Briggs to finalize the design so that full production could commence initially at Dagenham, then at Doncaster. Palmer recalled numerous trips to Dagenham with Callcott Reilly, mercilessly thrashing the latter's Citroën Light Fifteen up and down the old Great North Road. The 400-mile (650km) round trip would generally be done within a single day, and of course, the A1 at that time threaded its way through many villages and towns, so the journey was no pushover. Later, the Citroën was replaced with a prototype Javelin, thus providing additional testing opportunities.

Another rare Kodak Brownie-type snapshot. This, the third prototype, was fitted with a plastic one-piece windscreen. (Mike Kember)

Briggs Doncaster

Almost all Javelin and Bradford van bodies were constructed, painted and trimmed at the Carr Hill (Doncaster) factory of Briggs Motor Bodies.

The Riverside plant at Dagenham, the Briggs main facility, was at various times heavily involved with body production for other car makers, notably of course for major shareholder Ford but also Austin, Rootes, Standard, Riley, Leyland and Chrysler. On the outbreak of World War II, the company was approached by the British government to undertake multifarious production of items ranging from steel helmets and deep-sea mine sinkers to ammunition boxes and aircraft components.

Owing to continued enemy bombing, however, the decision was taken in November 1940 to convert the London and North Eastern Railway (LNER) carriage works at Doncaster into a production facility. The original Carr Hill building had been erected in 1889. In November 1942 Carr Hill was extended to some 227,000sq ft (21,000sq m), spread over an 8 acre (3.2ha) site, and continued making Halifax and Mosquito aircraft engine parts as well as automotive body assemblies. By March 1942 a total of 200 Lancaster cowlings per week (enough for fifty aircraft) were being produced.

Almost 23,000 Javelin bodies (and probably more than 35,000 Bradfords) came out of Carr Hill, to be transported by road to Idle.

Briggs sold the factory in 1964 to International Harvester (later J. I. Case Tractors), and it is currently owned by Graziano Gears who make and export transmission assemblies for the agricultural industry. Many features of the original 1889 building still exist, in particular the cast-iron pillars and roof trusses. When the original carriage works conversion took place in 1940, the railway lines were merely concreted over. This posed problems much later when Case tractors installed a wire-guided pallet carrier system. Unfortunately, the automated pallets developed a habit of following the old rails rather than their intended course!

Gerald Palmer tries out the second prototype on White Horse Bank near Thirsk. (Palmer)

Prepared for the Motoring Cavalcades, EAK 771 was the first Javelin widely seen by the motoring public. This car still displays the early rear wing and bumper styling. (JCC)

Massive efforts were made to prepare a car for the Society of Motor Manufacturers and Traders' (SMMT) Cavalcade of Motoring on 27 July 1946, a truly magnificent motoring pageant for vehicles of all ages, commencing with a display in London's Regent's Park attended by Their Royal Highnesses King George VI and Queen Elizabeth. This was followed by a demonstration parade through Park Lane, Piccadilly, Shaftesbury Avenue and Oxford Street. Crowds lined the route ten deep in places – indeed, a major criticism of the event came from those members of the public who could not see the action. Jowett had one of their original tiller-steering cars at the forefront of the parade, but most eyes were on Javelin EAK 771, one of the last prototypes that,

EAK again, this time in the Scottish Cavalcade. (JCC)

for the first time, had been hurriedly fitted with a Triplex curved windscreen specially for the show. Jowett had been approached by Triplex of Birmingham with the offer of supplying this new 'invention', and readily accepted the opportunity of displaying what would now be the first British production car with such a screen. A slightly curved, wider rear window was also made available for subsequent installation on later cars.

The Cavalcade Javelin drew enormous interest from an excited public. Many pictures of the new Jowett that had hitherto appeared in motoring journals were merely of a wooden scale model, which still exists in the hands of the JCC (Jowett Car Club). The mock registration number was JCL 341 (Jowett Cars Ltd – telephone Bradford 341).

Because of the 'Americanized' profile, many people had imagined that the car would be of American proportions and were somewhat bemused by how small it was in reality. The compact external dimensions belied the interior room, however, as we shall see elsewhere in this story. In its comprehensive review of the parade the following week *The Autocar* captioned a photograph of EAK thus: 'Spectators were puzzled and then surprised by the discovery that this was the 1946 Jowett. It created a good impression.'

Interestingly the London Cavalcade was filmed by the BBC in one of its very early outside broadcast productions. The event was reinforced by similar but rather more modest cavalcades held in Manchester and Glasgow later that year. Indeed, the SMMT was very active at this time in promoting British car manufacturers, and subsequently organized an impressive Jubilee Exhibition at 148 Piccadilly, an event that had been attended by more than 30,000 visitors by the time it closed on 10 August.

Preparing the Car for Mass Production

Frantic work proceeded on readying the car for mass production – and of course the amount of preparation at Briggs had to be paralleled at Idle, because a purpose-built assembly line would be required. It will be appreciated that the bodies as delivered from Briggs, although painted and trimmed, had no mechanical components fitted. Furthermore an engine manufacturing and assembly facility would also be required.

April 1947 saw the appointment of Frank Salter MIME, formerly with Daimler, General Motors and Standard, as consulting production engineer. Salter became a great asset to Jowett owing to his intelligent and innovative approach to production facility design issues, and whilst design details of the Javelin were being finalized he developed the production line for the Bradford van, soon being turned out at a rate of one every nineteen minutes. In co-ordination with George King Ltd of Peterborough, Salter went on to oversee the installation of a novel inverting cage mechanized assembly feature that facilitated the fixing of mechanical components to the up-turned Javelin bodies. The overall layout of the production facilities won considerable praise for the skilful utilization of available space.

Frustrating delays of one sort or another affected the project, which is hardly surprising, given the relative short supply of funding and personnel, the shortage of raw materials and the complexity of the design. Skilled engineers in particular were hard to come by following the ravages of war. In retrospect, that the car ever reached production is something of a minor miracle. But dogged determination won the day, and by mid-1947 a few started to trickle through. Even by this time, however, the Briggs Doncaster facility was not ready to build Javelin bodies; indeed, the first 639 carcasses came from the overcrowded Dagenham plant. Doncaster-built bodies would not start flowing until early 1948.

An indication of this slow start is that some time previously a London showroom had been established at 48 Albermarle Street, run by the enthusiastic John Baldwin; but for far too long Baldwin had little to display other than a couple of Bradford vans and a small scale model of the Javelin.

A massive task was put in place to appoint and train dealers and mechanics, almost 250 British

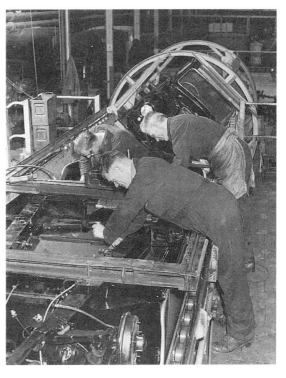

Novel Javelin production line at Idle. This March 1952 photo shows the Javelin body being inverted. (Woods Visual Imaging)

Suspension and other underside components being fitted. (Woods Visual Imaging)

Javelins nearing completion: this photo was taken in July 1950. A Bradford van line can be seen in the background. (Woods Visual Imaging)

The 1½ litre Jowett JAVELIN

ITS   NEW   RIGHT   THROUGH

A 1947 advertising image of the Javelin. (JCC)

agents being commissioned, with a further ninety-two selected in sixty-five overseas countries. Week-long courses for garage staff were held in a wooden-built 'training school' at the bottom end of the factory site so they could be familiarized not only with repair techniques, but also the construction methods employed in building the cars. Some local dealers stayed longer and spent time on the production line. Local bed and breakfast establishments were said to prosper as a result. Franco Morandi, the son of a Swiss agent who had a Jowett agency in Lugano, spent a whole year at the factory. On his return, Franco (who was apparently an accomplished driver) would often take a demonstration Javelin along the Ticino Valley to the foot of the St Gotthard Pass, then take great delight in chasing and beating other cars to the summit, whereupon a sign would be displayed inviting the drivers of the vanquished cars to invest in a new Javelin. Apparently a number of sales resulted from this innovative technique.

Jowett's own people also had to learn, among other things, how the cars would be affected by road accident damage. To this end, a complete Javelin was dropped nose first onto concrete from a gantry outside the factory fire station. Accident repair at the factory subsequently provided quite lucrative business, since the car seemed to attract drivers with a propensity to drive up to, and beyond, the cars' abilities. This could have been influenced by advertising campaigns that included phrases such as: 'Take a good look when it passes you' and 'A clear patch and you put your foot down in third ... travelling fast – 60, 65, 70, 75. You work out your average (speed), it's high. This car grips a bend and straightens it out...', and so on.

EAK outside the London showroom – but no Javelins inside! (JCC)

Accident repair at the factory became a lucrative business due to over-enthusiastic drivers. (JCC)

Foreign Manufacturers Take Note

It is hardly surprising, then, that Jowett's new car attracted not only the hungry attentions of journalists and motoring enthusiasts, but also a number of foreign manufacturers (notably in America), who sat up and took careful note. Javelin D8 PA 44 was shipped to the Chrysler Corporation who comprehensively tested and dissected it. A lengthy report was produced, dated 20 October 1948, which was largely complimentary; indeed some of the Javelin design features (such as the hexagonal-ended torsion bars) subsequently found their way onto Chrysler's own cars. Here is the preface to the report, and some of the things the report had to say:

> Since the Jowett Javelin was the first especially interesting post-war British car to be produced, one was obtained for demonstration and engineering test. The car was driven by personnel of the various laboratories.
>
> … The various systems (braking, steering, suspension and so on) of the Jowett Javelin are generally satisfactory. The torsion bar suspension used both front and rear gives a well balanced ride, considering the weight of the car.
>
> … It is recommended that the steering knuckle and knuckle support be examined to determine whether they merit consideration for light weight, simplicity and rugged design.
>
> … Brake tests showed the car to have brake performance comparable to present Chrysler products... current American cars develop a pedal pressure of 200lb in approx. ten stops from 50mph [80km/h], while the Javelin develops a pedal pressure of 200lb in approx. fifteen stops from 50mph.
>
> ...Steering characteristics are good. The car had a straight level ride, even on bumpy roads, with negligible wheel fight. Rear wheel steering was practically non-existent. Stability on curves was good also.

Chrysler's technical analysis of the Javelin was quite involved, running to thirty pages and including photographs, drawings and technical graphs. It assessed the car in what was called a 'shake test', wherein it was driven on a rough course for several miles at 60mph (100km/h). Pedometers were attached to the body to record vertical and horizontal deflections; these were then compared (quite favourably) with a Plymouth P15. Other detailed tests even extended to measuring the hardness of the engine-mounting rubbers. It is doubtful that Jowett themselves had gone to these extremes!

Three other US firms bought Javelins for examination. One was Studebaker, who took D8 PA 45, Ford had a look at D8 PA 46 and Nash Kelvinator subsequently bought D9 PBL 6189. It is curious that Chrysler, Studebaker and Ford ended up owning three consecutively numbered cars: clearly some sort of 'deal' was involved. Could Jowett have been instructed to share the Javelin's secrets with the Americans in the same way that Frank Whittle's jet engine design was revealed to them?

The Javelin's Impact at Home

To fully appreciate the Javelin's impact back in Great Britain, it is worth considering what a few motoring periodicals had to say, early in the car's production life:

> *The Autocar*, May 1947:
> A complete break with tradition …
> Accommodation for passengers and the appearance are indeed imposing …
> A design that bristles with novelty…
> In short, the Javelin is an entirely new and advanced design that can truly be described as a post-war model that has no direct association with 1939 and all that …

> *The Motor*, July 1949
> Offering outstanding performance, economy and comfort for rough roads…
> Abnormally good performance…
> Remarkable passenger space on a wheelbase of moderate dimensions. The Jowett is outstandingly comfortable on rough roads at all speeds. The performance on corners … is considerably

World-Wide Acclaim!

Extract from a letter to *The Motor,* dated 25 February 1953:

Contrary to the usual trend, my Jowett Javelin De-Luxe is adequately supplied with tools that are really useful. They are chrome-plated, neatly stowed away in a tool tray free from the entry of rain and floodwaters, and are quickly accessible without having to heave all the baggage out first!

Because of their robustness, I give instructions to our local garages to use them in preference to their 'V'-shaped jaw spanners! … Likewise I found the grease gun, although not intended for frequent use, perfectly satisfactory for my 9,000-mile [14,500km/h] Scandinavian tour in 1951.

FHG Wagner, Ipoh,
Perak,
Malaya.

And from another overseas owner, this time in *The Autocar,* of 2 October 1953:

Having just returned from a 3,400-mile [5,550km/h] touring holiday trip in France, Switzerland and Italy, my 1950 Javelin gave me an average fuel consumption of 29mpg [9.8ltr/100km]. During my trip the car climbed on five occasions well above 6,600ft [2,000m], and it was carrying four passengers and a lot of luggage. All normal main road passes were climbed in top or third gears (Susten Pass 7,400ft [2,260m], Oberalp Pass 6,700ft [2,000m], Lukmanier Pass 6,300 ft [1,920m]). The cruising speed was always around 55mph [88km/h] and a top speed of 85mph [137km/h] was recorded on the Milano-Como autostrada.

Adriano Pascucci
Barcelona
Spain

Carlton Coachworks drophead Javelin of 1948. The decision not to proceed with this design cleared the way for the Jupiter project. (Geoff McAuley)

*Worblaufen Javelin
exhibited at the Geneva
Motor Show in March
1951 (LAT
Photographic)*

superior to the normal family saloon.

The steering column gear lever ... may be considered a model of its kind ...

A high performance small car which will stand the most searching comparison with products of any other country.

Clearly, Jowett now had a car that would appeal to markets world-wide: 'It's new right through', the advertisements proclaimed. 'Take a good look when it passes you', and 'This car is a waste of money if you don't care what a car *does*.'

What was claimed to be the first Javelin to come off the production line (FAK 111) was taken by Callcott Reilly on a sales tour of Switzerland, Belgium and Holland on 19 November 1947. An early production model, FAK 573, was driven first to the Brussels Salon in February 1948 and then to the Geneva Motor Show in March. The same car was tested by *The Autocar*, and was photographed for a series of magazine advertisements (some in colour). Jowett chairman George Wansbrough and Callcott Reilly took FAK 698 to New York aboard the liner Queen Elizabeth, and then drove to Detroit and Windsor Ontario.

The London Motor Show of 1948 had provided Jowett with an immensely popular show-

case, with a Golden Sand (Tampico Beige) and a Turquoise saloon on show. Also on display was a maroon drophead version of the car, produced following an idea of Callcott Reilly and Gordon England, and constructed by Carlton Coachworks. It was a slightly awkward design, but not dissimilar in shape to certain American variations on this theme. Despite the integral chassis of the Javelin saloon's body, the drophead lacked the rigidity of a Javelin saloon. No further dropheads were produced, although this car was rescued and magnificently restored in the late nineties by JCC member Dennis Cremer. One other drophead Javelin, of slightly nicer proportions, appeared at the Geneva Show in 1951, this time from the Swiss coachbuilder Worblaufen.

The quest now was to make an impression on the world marketplace, and so achieve the exports that would be vital to ensure the allocation of sufficient quantities of steel. Overseas markets were now starting to bear fruit, and for some parts of the world, cars were being prepared in 'complete knock down' (CKD) form, for reassembly at their foreign destination.

By the time of the 1949 London Show, the Jupiter was also in prospect, and ever more interest was being shown in the products from Idle. The question was, could it be sustained?

3 A Journey Through the Javelin

As we have observed, a Javelin advertisement encouraged one to 'Take a good look when it passes you.' So, on the basis that the reader is viewing the Javelin from behind, this is where we'll start our journey! Our quest is to discover the things that made the Javelin rather special.

The Javelin from Behind

Open the boot lid and you'll hear a mechanical clunk as it nears its fully opened position. Then look closely at the top middle of the opening, at the cleverly designed over-centre leaf-spring arrangement that secures the lid in an open position. To close the boot, just press down on the lid (or if the resulting noise offends, push down the tab on the spring to release the pressure first).

For the moment though, let's leave the boot lid open. Despite the car's sloping tail, the boot itself is quite box-shaped, helped somewhat by the concave shape of the lid.

Peer down towards the outer edge of the floor and you'll see a sliding clip which, when withdrawn, allows access to a two-tier tool chest. The upper level has a handy moulded tray securely holding spanners, screwdriver and other small tools. The tray can be pulled clear of the chest and carried away. In the felt-covered lid of the chest can be found a few more small tools held neatly in small stitched pouches. Beneath the upper tray is a compartment for larger items such as the starting handle, jack, wheel brace and grease gun.

To the right-hand side of the lower tray is a large brass nut, connected to a lead-screw. This is designed to be operated with the wheel

The useful dual-tray toolbox fits neatly into the tail. The upper tray can be removed. Turning the large nut with the wheelbrace lowers the spare wheel carrier. (Geoff McAuley)

brace, and lowers a hidden under-boot cradle housing the spare wheel. Because this cradle is enclosed, the spare wheel will be clean and pristine when removed. (Sadly, later models used an open cradle that doesn't protect the spare quite so well.)

By now it will have been observed that there is no intrusion of the rear suspension into the boot area (how many current cars can make that claim?); this is due to the clever use of laterally positioned torsion bars between the boot bulkhead and the rear seat cushion. Two pairs of parallel arms locate the back axle, assisted by a diagonally positioned Panhard rod, and none of these items intrudes into the boot area.

In the Back

A little farther forward now and we're inside the car. Note that the rear seat (on most models) has a comfortable fold-away centre armrest, and for the outboard elbows, two more armrests. However, in cognizance of the Javelin's proclaimed six-seater capabilities, these outer ones conveniently slide out of their retaining pouches for occasions when full seat width is desired.

If you're fortunate enough to be sitting in a de Luxe version of the car, you will notice two small hollow brackets in front of you on the rear of the front seat. Turning round now, you will find a full-width picnic shelf neatly shaped to fit in the area underneath the rear window: this can be pulled away from its nesting place and slotted into the aforementioned brackets. The picnic can now commence!

To sit on there is a comfortable seat cushion; this can easily be removed by pulling upwards from its base, and underneath will be found a wooden compartment lid: here is housed the 12-volt battery (one 6-volt battery on either side for earlier models). Like the spare wheel, this is mounted low in the car, thus helping to keep the centre of gravity where it is most wanted. Whilst the seat is out, those clever torsion bars can be admired.

Replacing the seat and climbing aboard the car, it's worth noting how light and airy the Javelin seems. This is helped to no small degree by the rearmost side windows, positioned in just the right place to watch the world speed by.

Easily removable armrests allow three-abreast seating. (Geoff McAuley)

Transverse torsion bars hide behind the rear seat cushion. (Geoff McAuley)

On our way to investigating the front seat, we pass the mid-positioned jacking points. These hollow square tubes are designed to accept the Stephenson jack, which is operated by the wheel brace. A few rotations of the brace lifts the whole of one side of the car and, to stress how easy this is, Jowett's advertising showed a delicate lady exe-cuting the operation, wearing a contented smile and her best summer dress. Today we would call that 'sexist' – but also today, our poor lady driver would be on her hands and knees struggling with an inadequate and fiddly scissor jack. Hardly a suitable scenario for a manufacturer's glossy brochure!

The chromed handle on the front seat adjusts the reach and rake in one go. (Geoff McAuley)

In the Front

Round to the front of the car now, and – choosing to ignore the rather ludicrous semaphore indicators of the period – we settle into the bench front seat. Again, on most models we have a comfortable, fold-away, centre armrest, and unlike many younger cars, this happens to be positioned ideally for the elbows of both driver and passenger. As was the case in the rear, the other elbows aren't forgotten, but this time in the interests of three-abreast seating, the door-mounted armrests fold neatly against the door panel, and are secured by large press studs.

Depending on the model, the bench seat is adjusted for reach and rake by ingenious mechanisms. A ratcheted sliding bar arrangement is fitted to early cars, to be later replaced by an infinitely variable lead-screw version, controlled by a rather classy chromium-plated, centre-mounted handle. In both cases, as the seat slides backwards, the backrest automatically tilts, relying on an assumption that drivers with long legs are also endowed with long arms. The other front occupant(s), of course, has (have) no say in the matter!

On later models, the starter solenoid (with manual override button) is handily placed on the floor just ahead of the seat adjuster. Again on some models a twelve-volt socket outlet is fitted adjacent to the solenoid button. The days of utilizing the cigarette (cigar) lighter for powering ancillary equipment were not yet prevalent.

Sharing the front seat with two (preferably lean) front passengers, the driver is aware of the advantage of the column-mounted gearchange. The stubby handbrake lever dips from below the offside of the dashboard, and the shortness and forward positioning of the engine and gearbox permit a flat floor – all of these things ensuring that six legs can be accommodated side by side.

On each side of the front scuttle is a small air vent flap: this rather cleverly takes in fresh air from the front of the car through a hollow strengthening member that forms part of the inner wing. The earliest cars had an operating lever that controlled both vents together, but later models provided an individual – and difficult to reach – handle on each flap.

Whilst exploring the depths of the footwell area, it may be pondered that there seems to be little space for the steering mechanism. Indeed, space is quite tight owing to the narrowness of the toe-board and the closeness of the engine/gearbox assembly. But Palmer's design of this item is typically inventive and practical: a small, crescent-shaped enclosure beneath the toe-board houses a compact gear and pinion assembly, with a cleverly shaped cross-arm channel that curves over the bell housing. The gear and pinion solution provides great economy of space, but gives the steering the accuracy associated with a rack and pinion system. Firm location points and short steering arms give the Javelin nicely weighted and accurate steering characteristics and a fairly good turning circle. This one area of design typifies the amazing ability of Palmer to 'think outside the box', as we would describe it today.

Before extricating oneself from the footwell exploration, it will be noted that the gearbox oil can be checked and replenished by the removal of a small cover underneath the carpet.

Under the Bonnet

Head under the bonnet now, and here the Javelin design gets really interesting. First, note the low and forward placement of the engine: that low

The low-slung engine helps ensure a low centre of gravity. (Geoff McAuley)

mounting position is again helping to achieve a healthy centre of gravity. The radiator, it will be observed, is mounted behind the engine, and to ensure a satisfactory air flow, vent holes are pressed into the inner wing area behind it (Palmer didn't want bonnet louvres, since he thought they would spoil the car's appearance).

Find the twin carburettors snuggling away in the depths of the engine bay. Can't see them properly? Then swing up the hinged front grill, or unscrew the handy knurled securing thimbles and remove the grill completely (the later, two-piece, cast aluminium grill was slightly less convenient than the early car's one-piece chromed brass strip affair). Now the carburettors can be seen more clearly, as can the part-metal, part-rubber air-feed tubes connected to them.

Follow the line of these tubes skywards, and it will be seen that when the bonnet is lowered, they connect via a pair of rubber trumpets into a wooden baffle mounted in the nose of the bonnet. This is the airbox, a complicated affair comprising silencing baffles and a sophisticated oil-bath filter.

Javelin Models, 1947–53

General:

All-steel four-door saloon body of unitary construction with integral box-section chassis.
Interior fitted with bench seats front and rear; passenger capacity three front and three rear.
Boot capacity: 9.75cu ft (1cu m).
Maximum overall load: 910lb (412kg).

Production life with delivery dates:

PA: first D8 PA 1 – 16 April 1948, last D9 PA 5206 – 12 October 1949.
PB: first D9 PB 5198 – 30 September 1949, last EO PB 11289 – 23 October 1950.
PC: first EO PC 11270 – 30 October 1950, last E1/PC19063 – 9 November 1951.
PD: first EI PDL 18995 – 10 January 1952, last E2 PD 22582 – 26 August 1952.
PE: first E2/PE/22450 – 1 September 1952, last E3/PE/24732 – 8 October 1953.
Total number of cars built: 23,307 approximately.

Engine*:*

Four cylinder horizontally opposed overhead valve. Die-cast aluminium two-piece cylinder block with cast-iron, wet liners.
Crankshaft mounted in steel-back shell bearings, front and centre copper/lead/indium, rear white metal with integral thrust faces.
Valves pushrod operated from central cast-iron camshaft. Zero-lash hydraulic tappets on early cars, later replaced with solid versions (from E0 PC 11907).
Twin Zenith carburettors with bonnet-mounted air cleaner.
AC mechanical fuel pump.
Pressure-fed lubrication from sump-mounted oil pump driven by worm gear on crankshaft.
Coil and contact breaker ignition.

Cooling by pressurized water system with belt-driven water pump incorporating cooling fan on extension shaft.
Water radiator mounted to rear of engine. Oil cooler optional.
Crankcase breather recirculatory.

Engine dimensions and capacities:

Bore and stroke: 72.5 × 90mm
Swept volume: 1,486cc
Compression ratio: 7.2:1
Maximum power: 50bhp at 4,100rpm (1949), then 52.5bhp at 4,500rpm,
Maximum torque 76lb-ft at 2,600rpm
Fuel tank: 8gallons (36 litres)

Clutch*:*

Borg & Beck: 7.25in single dry plate

Gearbox*:*

Four forward ratios plus reverse. Constant load synchromesh on second, third and top. Higher geared intermediate ratios from September 1951. Steering column gearchange.

Dimensions*:*

Wheelbase: 102in (2,591mm).
Track: 51in (1,295mm) front, 49in (1,245mm) rear.
Overall length: 168in (4,268mm).
Overall width: 61in (1,550mm).
Kerb weight: 2,258lb (1,023kg).

Steering:

Internal gear and pinion steering box 2.75 turns lock to lock.
Average turning circle 31ft 9in (9.7m).

The Javelin and the Jupiter benefit from Palmer's fastidious attention to accurate wheel location. Both the camber and the castor of the frontwheels are adjustable with specially designed shims. But another important requirement is ensuring that, as the steered wheels rise and fall under the influence of the suspension, the relative toe in/toe out is not affected by the positional variation between the inner and outer steering arm joints.

In order to minimize corruption of the all-important Ackerman geometry, adjustable-height 'track rod end' joints are incorporated which, with the aid of a simple gauge described in the Workshop Manual, permit the best compromise settings to be achieved to compensate for bump and rebound suspension movement. These adjustments permit accurate steering despite the cars' substantial suspension travel, thereby ensuring comfort with precision, a much praised feature of both saloon and convertible.

Front suspension:

Independent, unequal length parallel wishbone with longitudinal torsion bars. Metal bushed front suspension from outset, rubber bushed from chassis E2PD 21868.
Telescopic shock absorbers.

Rear suspension:

Four parallel trailing arms with transverse torsion bars. Panhard rod located from axle bracket. Telescopic shock absorbers. Live axle with Salisbury hypoid bevel.
Final-drive ratio 4.875 providing 15.5mph (25km/h) per 1,000rpm in top gear.

Wheels:

Steel disc 3-l6in, fitted with 5.25-16in cross-ply tyres (5.50-16in on de Luxe models).

Brakes:

Girling hydro-mechanical.
Cast iron hub/drum assemblies 9in (229mm) diameter.
Front single-leading, single-trailing shoes width 1.5in (38mm), hydraulically operated.
Rear shoe width 1.25in (31.75mm) mechanically-operated by rod from master cylinder body.
From chassis E0 PB 10594: Girling full hydraulic twin leading shoes at front, leading/trailing shoes at rear, width 1.75in (44.5mm) shoe width all round.
Handbrake to rear brakes by cable and rod from lever and ratchet under the dashboard.

Electrics:

Two 6-volt batteries in series, mounted under rear seat cushion (one 12-volt from D9 PA 3696).
Lucas headlamps PA/PB models 5.25in (133mm), PC/PD/PE models 7in (178mm) with double dipping filaments.

Performance:

Acceleration: 0–60mph (97km/h) in 22.2s, standing ¼ mile 22.7s, 40–60 in top 11.8s
Max. speed: 77.6mph (124.8km/h).
Consumption: 25.5mpg (11.0l/100km) (*The Motor*, July 1949).
0–60mph in 20.9s, standing ¼ mile 21.5s, 40-60 in top 13.9s.
Consumption: 29.lmpg (9.75l/100km).
Max. speed: 82.4mph (132km/h) (*The Motor*, April 1953).

Specification and Price by Year

1948–49: Single model, metal dash with rectangular instruments (speedometer, water temperature and fuel), leather seats with armrests front and rear. Heater. Colours: light grey with red upholstery. Pale beige with brown cloth or leather upholstery. Black with red leather. UK retail price (1948) £718.53 (basic price £640.00). Radio £42.21 (basic £31.975).

1949–50: Standard saloon, sliding front seat adjustment, metal dash with rectangular instruments as before, single sun visor. Heater optional. Colours: Tampico beige or sage green, with beige plastic or cloth upholstery. UK retail price £761.03 (basic £595.00). Radio £37.09 (basic £28.10). Saloon de Luxe, as for standard saloon, but with picnic tray, heavy section bumpers, spotlight, walnut veneer wooden dashboard with additional oil pressure gauge and ammeter. Colours: black with brown hide upholstery. Turquoise or maroon with beige hide. Metallic grey with red hide. UK retail price £933.71 (basic £732.10).

1950–51: Standard saloon, new-type two-piece aluminium grille with different bonnet trim. Colours: Connaught green or Tampico beige with beige plastic upholstery. UK retail price: November 1950, £761.03 (basic £595). Saloon de Luxe, grille and bonnet trim as for basic model. Roof-mounted aerial. Colours as before. UK retail price £888.80 (basic £695).

1951–52: Standard saloon, metal dashboard now has circular instruments. Oil cooler. No armrests. Colours black or Tampico beige with beige plastic upholstery. UK retail price: August 1951, £989.275 (basic £635). Saloon de luxe, revised dashboard with chrome bezel instruments including clock. Oil cooler. Tyres 550-16in. Colours black, golden sand metallic, gunmetal grey metallic, maroon metallic. Price: August 1951, £1,144.83 (basic £735).

1953: Models as for 1952. Prices Javelin saloon (standard) November 1952 £1,082.61 (basic £695), 1953 £886.54 (basic £625); de Luxe November 1952, £1,207.05 (basic £775), 1953 £957.375 (basic £675).

Very little else in the engine bay will seem familiar. The whole layout is compact in the extreme, and shows a fine degree of original design thinking. Minor criticisms concern rather poor access to the sparking plugs (although rumours that a road wheel must be removed to get at the plugs are incorrect), and a rather narrow footwell due to the 'cab forward' design – an almost inevitable downside of maximizing interior space to such an extent.

These, then, are some of the more obvious flashes of genius to be found in our Javelin. There are many other minor design details, often hidden within the depths of the car's oily bits, but nonetheless contributing to a vehicle that is quite outstanding in its cleverness of conception. It is interesting to note that, in the twenty-first century, designers of compact cars are turning again to the concepts of space utilization that can be found in the Javelin.

Split front grille of the later model. Note the oil-bath air filter cleverly located in the nose of the bonnet. (Geoff McAuley)

4 The Javelin Comes of Age

Confidence was in abundance. It is hardly surprising that individuals with an interest in motor sport sat up and took notice, despite the fact that the design team had intended no sporting potential. The well-known competition driver and garage owner Tommy Wise (see the panel on page 42, penned by Tommy's son Tim) was one of the first to appreciate the likelihood that the new car could be a competitive rally car. On 7 October 1948 he took delivery of a Javelin (D8 PA 682 registered MNW 444) in order to enter the first post-war Monte Carlo Rally the following January. He invited another car dealer, T.C. (Cuth) Harrison to join him, and in a clever move to have some technical expertise on board, Palmer was persuaded to come along as second co-driver.

Monte Carlo Rally 1949

There had been no Monte Carlo Rally since before the war. An abortive attempt had been made to run the event in 1948, but fuel restrictions in France had led to its cancellation. The year 1949 was to prove more successful, however, and drew an entry list of 205 cars, almost one quarter of this total electing to start from Glasgow. This 'local' venue allowed the Jowett crew to stop off en route for 'a nice cup of tea and a sandwich'.

The organizers had set an average speed requirement of 31mph (50km/h) for the three day/three night journey. But on the assumption that this alone would provide a tough enough challenge to deplete the field, no special tests were held until the principality was reached. Since the weather was mild, however, rather more competitors than expected survived to tackle the

final eliminating trial. This was a demanding regularity run of three 17.5km laps of a road circuit in the mountains above Monaco taken after just one night's rest. The circuit was supposed to be kept secret until the start, although every monégasque taxi driver seemed to know it. It was divided into two 3km sections that had to be completed as fast as possible and in exactly the same time, and a 10km length to be covered at an average of at least 30mph (50km/h). After one practice lap, two were timed, and every 1 second difference was penalized one point. The test favoured the fastest cars, the bravest drivers, those with multiple stopwatches, and those who had been able to squeeze in some practice.

Palmer later recalled the event with both awe and admiration in equal measure. He had no idea that his car could be driven with such verve and aggression, but at the end of this gruelling rally, MNW 444 came home to win the 1,500cc class (fourteenth overall) from over 200 starters, and beating the well known Dutch rallyist Maurice Gatsonides (later of Gatso speed-camera fame) into second place. This result only prevailed because Palmer noticed a mistake by the organizers, who had calculated the Jowett team's time wrongly. So his inclusion in the crew had been thoroughly vindicated! Strangely, Palmer's discovery of the error was officially accepted only after the presentation ceremony; the Riviera Cup and £75 prize money was already with Gatsonides when the altered result was announced, and whilst the Dutchman reluctantly handed back the cup, he claimed that the money had already been spent, leaving the organizers with no option but to come up with another £75! Gatso later grumbled that the Jowett crew's objection should

Tommy Wise

One of the names that keeps cropping up in this new book on Jowetts is that of my father, Tommy (TC) Wise, and I am honoured to have been asked by the authors to write a few words about him and his contacts with Jowetts.

Before the war, TC was heavily involved in trialling and mud-plugging, first in 1933 with a fearsome Ford V8-engined beast bought from his friend Sydney Allard, and which was possibly the first Allard. Between then and 1939 he competed all over Britain in a series of Ford V8 devices (none of which cost more than £17.50p) with considerable success, and many of his trophies are still in the family.

After the war he built two trials specials, each with a huge Mercury V8 plus a lot of 'added lightness', registered JUG 3 and KUM 444. It was at this time that he teamed up with T.C. 'Cuth' Harrison, a Ford dealer from Sheffield, who did the 1949 Monte with him together with Gerry Palmer in Tommy's own Javelin MNW 444. The story goes that Gerry actually spent most of the rally curled up on the rear floor of the Javelin in the foetal position, especially when the two TCs were pressing on! This shows the space available in the rear of this family saloon! The 444 registration numbers were chosen to commemorate my birth date in April 1944, and also gave the name to the 4/44 Trophy Trial, run to this day by the Yorkshire Sports Car Club. Tommy's expertise on the slippery muddy stuff stood him in good stead for driving on the slippery icy stuff.

Nikki Wise, Tommy's daughter, proudly displays the Riviera Cup surrendered by Gatsonides. (Geoff McAuley)

I well remember the Jupiters from the tender age of six, in particular the ex-Le Mans GKW 111 all stripped out and used as a road car as well as for racing and rallying at international level – just imagine doing that with the same car nowadays! I also remember being picked up from school in Scarborough by T.C. in a rather snub-nosed Jupiter (possibly one of the Monte GKY series) that he had managed to stuff through a hedge after headlight failure (so he said!) on a particularly twisty bit of road near the A1. Not being able to find a way out of the ploughed field in the dark and with no headlights, he created another hole in the hedge, and proceeded to Scarborough with a little more decorum. The two holes in the hedge were there for many years afterwards. Perhaps that is why Jupiters have the radiator behind the engine!

There is also the story, possibly apocryphal, of T.C. and Mike Wilson almost getting themselves thrown out of the hotel in Le Mans 1950 after an episode involving Mike sitting in the bathtub and being joined unceremoniously by an aspidistra including pot. Talking of Mike Wilson, T.C .always paid great tribute to his mathematical and navigating skills, saying he could put his head down and navigate for 24 hours on end, while Tommy could be at the wheel for the same length of time: there was total trust the one in the other. Mike's extra ballast (up to 24 stone when in his prime!) was well worth it, and history shows they made a successful team.

Many of these thoughts go through my head when I am driving my own Jupiter, and it makes me very proud to think that my father had so much to do with the early competition history of these cars.

Victors, the 1949 Monte Carlo Rally. Left to right: Cuth Harrison, Tommy Wise, Gerald Palmer. (JCC)

not have been accepted, but he did grudgingly concede that, morally at least, his Hillman had been beaten by the Jowett.

Five other Javelins had entered the rally, the best of the rest being the R. Smith, R. (Bob) Ellison and H. Schofield car that came third in class at twenty-second overall.

Spa Francorchamps 1949

Following the Monte success, motoring journalist Anthony Hume, who had also contested the rally, read with some disappointment that the Javelin had not received a great amount of attention at the Brussels show; he therefore asked the factory to consider entering a three-car team in the 24-hour race at Spa Francorchamps, to be held on 9 July 1949. It was decided that there would not be sufficient time to prepare three cars, but one production model would be made ready for Hume to drive. His chosen co-driver was Tom Wisdom. The car would be standard in most respects, although a higher compression engine, racing tyres and slightly higher overall gearing were allowed. As was common practice,

the Javelin was driven to the race, a good shake-down opportunity! Horace Grimley and Charles Grandfield travelled down in a back-up Javelin towing Grimley's holiday trailer full of spares.

The Spa circuit, whose 9-mile (14km) long dusty surface meandered through some of the finest forest scenery in the Ardennes, incorporated steep gradients and tricky corners, and was considered to be a considerably more difficult course than the better known Le Mans. This would be a harsh test for all the competing cars, drivers and mechanics. Leslie Johnson of English Racing Automobiles (ERA) Ltd was to drive a works 2.5 litre Aston Martin. The same Leslie Johnson figures elsewhere in our telling of the Jupiter story, and his presence in this race (and the effect that the Javelin's performance had upon him) may have been partly instrumental in the Jupiter ever being contemplated.

The event was to be started by echelon, wherein the drivers ran across the track to board their diagonally parked mounts. The story is told by Hume that Wisdom, who was taking the first stint, noticed that the car on his right, a BMW coupe driven by Marcel Masuy, was left-hand drive, and therefore the doors of the two cars might clash as the drivers scrambled to start the race. Wisdom slyly suggested to Masuy that, as the BMW was undoubtedly much faster, the Frenchman should go first. Hume continues, 'His Gallic courtesy to the fore, Masuy insisted that, as his extra speed would doubtless enable him quickly to overtake the Javelin, nothing would satisfy him but that "Monsieur Visdom" should have every advantage by going first.' This was clearly what the wily Wisdom had wanted all along and, disappearing like a rocket, the Javelin never encountered the BMW again during the race!

At 4 o'clock prompt, with a hot sun glaring from a cloudless blue sky, the rather undisciplined combatants impatiently raced off in a vast cloud of dust. At the end of lap one, the two 1,500cc Ecurie Gordini Simcas of Trintignant and Manzon led the field, closely followed by Chinetti's Ferrari. After the first hour the Javelin trailed the Van Malder/Nerinckx MG in the 2-litre touring car class; but within three hours, the Javelin was leading the class ahead of MG, Lancia and Citroën. The drivers and the pit crew were working 'like clockwork', despite the fact that the latter were in this role for the very first time. At the fourth hour the Javelin continued with the class lead, averaging 67.81mph (109.1km/h); another four hours and the Jowett's average had dropped a little to 66.44mph (106.9km/h) – but the Yorkshire car still headed its class.

The Jowett pit crew became alarmed when, on passing the pits in the fifth hour, Wisdom was observed striking the palm of his hand against the car door through the open window. The pit crew prepared for major problems at the next pit stop, but it transpired that the driver had merely been

Spa 24-hour race 1949 class winner: 'A nice little motor' (Tom Wisdom). (JCC)

Excellent pit work by the Jowett crew. (JCC)

communicating how well this 'nice little car' was performing!

After 12 hours the Chinetti/Lucas Ferrari was fastest overall at 78.99mph (127.09km/h), whilst Hume and Wisdom were three laps ahead of the second in class MG – remember, each lap was 9 miles (14km)! By the twenty-first hour, the Jowett team realized that with a little more pace they could win not only the 2-litre Touring Car class, but they could also beat the best of the 4-litre Touring Car class (Mesdame Rouault and Simon on a Delage). So the Javelin's speed was increased (while most other teams were easing off to ensure they would finish intact), and the Delage was duly beaten by some 28 miles (45km).

Chinetti in his Ferrari achieved the fastest overall speed, a record-breaking 76.61mph (123.3km/h), despite having spun off on spilt oil, pinning a spectator against a wall and breaking her leg. The driver administered first aid to the woman before continuing! The Javelin had averaged 65.5mph (110.7km/h), including all pit stops – probably at least ten in number – and had thereby covered a distance of 1,572 miles (2,534.5km). The most serious incident had been when Hume

snagged and broke a finger on the glove box lid.

The Coupe de la Victoire prize for the best placed British car was awarded to the Thompson/Fairman HRG, despite the fact that the Javelin had bettered the 'Hurg' by more than 9 miles. The HRG crew sportingly protested the error, but the organizers were adamant that no mistake had been made. Perhaps they just couldn't believe the Javelin's incredible result.

A Magnificent Performance

The Jowett and its drivers had performed magnificently, but the pit crew also came in for praise. Here is what *The Autocar* had to say:

> In racing, '*experientia docet*' is sometimes belied in more ways than one. For instance, at Spa last weekend, from all accounts, there was a striking contrast between the preparedness and good organization of the Jowett pit, manned by an inexperienced but thought-taking staff, and the relatively haphazard atmosphere in quarters dripping with '*experientia*'.
>
> Talking of the Javelin, whose performance made a very great impression in Belgium,

rumours have been going around to the effect that this car had a 'sports prototype' engine. These are quite untrue. The Hume/Wisdom machine had had its engine very exactingly assembled and the compression ratio was higher than standard to take advantage of the 'better than Pool' (though not much better) octane rating of Belgian petrol; apart from that and the rather sparse interior furnishings in the interest of lightness, the Javelin was regular. As a matter of fact, the ordinary wide-ratio gears were naturally a considerable handicap, because at places like the hill at L'Eau Rouge, which was taken in top, unwelcome dicing was necessary to avoid the need for a change-down'.

At this point it is perhaps timely to consider the performance figures for the Javelin, as recorded by one of the leading motoring journals, *The Motor*. British cars with 1,500cc engines were not particularly common at this time, although examples were to be found in the Morris Oxford, Riley 1½, Singer SM 1500, Vauxhall Wyvern and Wolseley 4/50. In 1949, *The Motor* recorded the figures given in Table 1 (page 48).

So, with the exception of the Riley's top speed, the Javelin was the considerably quicker car in the 1,500cc segment. Even if we consider cars with much larger engines, such as the Austin A70 Hampshire (2,199cc), the Humber Hawk (1,944cc), the Vauxhall Velox (2,275cc) and the Wolseley 6/80 (2,215cc), the Jowett holds its own quite impressively – *see* Table 2 (page 48).

Add to this the Javelin's nimble handling, and it is easy to understand why sporting types were attracted to it.

The London Motor Show, October 1949. The first public appearance of the Jupiter chassis. (JCC)

Javelin in the Monte Carlo Rally of 1950. (Collection Joves)

TABLE 1

Car	0-60mph	30-50mph (top gear)	Max. speed
Jowett Javelin	22.4sec	11.1sec	77.6mph (124.9km/h)
Morris	31.0sec	15.8sec	70.9mph (114.0km/h)
Riley	32.6sec	16.3sec	77.8mph (125.2km/h)
Singer	33.7sec	16.6sec	70.9mph (114.0km/h)
Vauxhall	N/A	18.4sec	60.0mph (96.5km/h)
Wolseley	31.6sec	17.1sec	74.2mph (119.4km/h)

TABLE 2

Car	0-60mph	30-50mph (top gear)	Max. speed
Austin A70	21.5sec	12.7sec	81.5mph (131.1km/h)
Humber	30.7sec	13.1sec	71.4mph (114.9km/h)
Vauxhall	22.7sec	9.8sec	73.5mph (118.2km/h)
Wolseley	27.8sec	15.1sec	76.9mph (123.7km/h)

Palmer's Misgivings

So, by the end of 1949 the Javelin was well established both as a fast, comfortable family car, and also as a very capable sporting saloon. The previous hectic six years had been a tremendous success for Palmer, and although history shows he subsequently produced many other worthy contributions throughout his career, his efforts during the period under discussion must rank as perhaps the most remarkably determined and productive for any individual car designer in history.

But despite the motor-racing successes, Palmer was increasingly troubled by the Jowett company's emphasis on sporting events. He knew the engine needed further development if it was to continue being used in this way, and although he took great satisfaction from the car's achieve-ments, the current situation was some way departed from his original brief to produce a utilitarian 'World Car'. At this time there were no firm plans to build a Javelin replacement, and the Jupiter had not yet evolved as a finished product.

Furthermore, his dear friend and colleague Callcott Reilly had been 'dismissed' by the board, and Palmer's adrenalin was probably waning following the mad years that had gone before.

It is therefore hardly surprising that, when approached by Nuffield to return to Oxford, he embraced the idea with not a little enthusiasm. After all, he was now a proven designer in high regard, and his future employment was hardly in doubt. In July 1949 Palmer and his family headed south for a new career in which he designed the MG Magnette, Wolseley 4/44, Riley Pathfinder and the Wolseley 6/90.

5 The Jupiter a Coachbuilder's Car

The Jupiter was the product of two quite separate and, one might think, opposite trains of thought. With the dramatic appearance of the Javelin on the sporting scene in 1949, some of the motor sportsmen of the time were beginning to cluster around Jowett, and to look for further works involvement from a management team that was still reluctant to become drawn into top-level competition. These people included Leslie Johnson of ERA Ltd; Laurence Pomeroy, the motoring journalist and technical editor of *The Motor*; Anthony Hume; Cuth Harrison, Yorkshire motor dealer and owner/racer of a very fast ERA; and Tom Wisdom and Tommy Wise whom we have met before and will meet again. It is no coincidence that four of these men had crewed either the Monte or the Spa Javelin. Not a strong theoretician, Charles Grandfield, the new engineering manager at Jowett, was attracted to the idea of racing to improve the breed: he saw experimentation as the way ahead for the new products at Idle.

ERA had begun producing single-seater racing cars in 1934 both for its works team and for sale to private entrants. These cars were mostly 1,100cc or 1,500cc supercharged (some double supercharged) and the roughly seventeen A, B, C and D types, in the famous hands of Raymond Mays, Prince Bira, Dick Seaman, Tony Rolt and several others, notched up around 120 wins and over ninety second places in international and national events up to 1939. ERAs were raced in almost all countries where motor sport then took place, and it is easy to see that, with successes like these, the name meant a great deal in British motor sporting circles in the late 1940s and early 1950s.

Leslie Johnson bought ERA Ltd in 1947 soon after its move to Dunstable. He asked the respected racing driver Bert Hadley to evaluate the factory cars, and on inspection, Hadley had little difficulty in persuading Johnson that they were obsolescent. As a consequence they were sold, a sound move because although in private hands they did continue to distinguish themselves for a time in Grands Prix and other events, it was obvious that they were becoming uncompetitive. Johnson therefore began two new ventures at ERA, the F-type Formula 3 and the G-type Formula 2, the latter evolving into the Bristol type 450 that took 1-2-3 in the 2-litre class at Le Mans in 1954. Another of Johnson's projects was to develop or build a 1,500cc sports racing car, and it looked as if the new Javelin had the essential ingredients. Anthony Hume was put in overall charge and he, Leslie Johnson and Pomeroy made representations to Jowett about ERA designing a sports car around Javelin mechanicals: it would be called the ERA-Javelin.

The Jowett board was mulling over a quite different consideration. The Javelin was beginning to sell in increasing numbers, but as we have already seen, it had hit a limitation – the availability of steel. The British government of the day was rationing that very scarce vital commodity to those companies with a good pre-war export record – and if you did not have much of a pre-war export record, you had to show current export orders. The burgeoning North American market did not seem to be taking up the Javelin in significant quantities, so a proposal was being considered for a two-seater sports car to take on the market being opened up jointly by MG and returning US servicemen.

The board was thinking along the lines of an up-to-date, luxury two-seater, clothed in all-enveloping drophead coachwork with all-weather protection, where the lowest possible weight was not the primary consideration. Compared with the MG TC it would have modern looks, modern equipment, modern appointments and comfort, and superior Javelin-derived ride and handling. It would sell at a higher price and generate higher unit profits, and most importantly extra steel for the Javelin.

By contrast, Johnson was thinking along the lines of a racing chassis with the power train, axles and suspension of the Javelin, the whole clothed in lightweight modern fixed-head coupé coachwork. Moreover, the ERA people had a chassis designer in mind, the Austrian-born Professor Dr Ing Robert Eberan-Eberhorst, the development engineer who tamed the fearsome Grand Prix Auto Unions of the immediate pre-war period. It was still remembered that these impressive German cars had trounced the ERAs at the Donington Grand Prix of October 1938. The professor was at this time in Italy working on the Cisitalia Grand Prix project, where his colleagues were no lesser figures than Ferry Porsche, Rudolph Hruska and Karl Abarth. Eberan had also recently been working on the Porsche 356 engine valve drive and combustion chambers, and had contributed to the chassis, suspension and general development of that car. But Cisitalia was fast running out of funding, and Eberan was looking for a career move.

Eberhorst taking notes at Nurburgring in 1939. (Nuvolari)

A Gentleman's Agreement and a New Chassis

Over an expensive lunch Leslie Johnson, a charmer of the first order, and Laurence Pomeroy somehow persuaded Jowett that there was enough common ground between the two concepts, and a gentleman's agreement was arrived at for five chassis, with a sixth retained by ERA for road-testing. It certainly helped having the technical editor of *The Motor* on hand! Eberhorst arrived in the summer of 1949 and got

directly to work, heading a small team that grew from one to four. A tubular chassis was designed, more sophisticated than any mass-producer would have attempted, so the new car began with a big advantage in roadholding. The frame comprised a pair of tubular longerons stoutly braced by a St Andrew's cross. A rigid triangulated structure of tubes carried the Javelin independent front suspension, while another similar structure at the rear carried the rear suspension and axle. Sturdy cross-tubes tied it all together. The Javelin layout of longitudinal front torsion bars and transverse rear ones, with live axle well located by trailing links and Panhard rod, was retained. The ERA-designed rack-and-pinion unit was incorporated and provided light and positive steering. Anti-roll bars were designed-in at both ends of the car, their main purpose being to reduce roll angles.

Artist's impression of the ERA-Javelin design. (Galleria di Tuttomotori)

A chassis was ready in time to be exhibited at the 1949 London Motor Show in October. A nearly complete car (there was no interior trim) with coupé coachwork, probably to the requirements of Johnson and Hume, was revealed at the Jowett London showroom, where it was admired by the motor-sporting world as advanced in concept. It was regarded as quite businesslike, resembling as it did several advanced racing coupés of the day. *Motor Sport* was enthusiastic:

> The announcement of a new tubular chassis high performance version of the well established Jowett Javelin, to be built by ERA and powered and serviced by Jowett, was one of September's greater excitements … on the ERA-Javelin the steering column has been lowered and the pedals set further back. The low side-members, torsion bars of modified rate, and anti-roll bars at each end of the chassis, together with heavy-duty Woodhead-Monroe shock absorbers and new rack-and-pinion steering gear, promise good road-holding and controllability.

As for the bodywork, the magazine continued:

> So trim, so refreshingly different did the car look … that those privileged to set eyes on the first complete ERA-Javelin were captivated.

Leslie Johnson, we are told by the magazine, had a personal interest in the new car.

However, Jowett were to have second thoughts and there was a parting of the ways. A bitterly disappointed Johnson was told that there would be no more chassis after the agreed five, no complete sports-racing car, and no engine development by Eberan. Jowett would build the chassis and design the coachwork, and all development work would be the responsibility of Charles Grandfield and his busy experimental department. This released Eberan, and off he went to design the chassis of the Aston Martin DB3 for David Brown, before returning to Germany to help re-found Auto Union and work on the revival of DKW.

Producing the Prototypes

Now it was Reg Korner's turn to get smartly to work, and he was given four months to turn the ERA-designed chassis into a complete motor car that Jowett felt would be bought by Americans; at the same time a lightweight version was required to meet the regulations for the 1950 Le Mans international 24-hour Grand Prix d'Endurance. Le Mans was the only European motor race that was seriously noticed in the United States in those days. In this way Jowett set out to meet both requirements outlined above in one machine! Korner worked night and day to achieve the deadline of two complete prototypes, one by the end of February 1950, and the Le

Mans racer by the following May.

During the design period, which included Christmas, his little daughter Joyce contracted meningitis, which was especially hard for Reg since his own sister had died from the disease. Joyce spent Christmas in hospital, and happily made a complete recovery.

The schedule of three complete cars and two exhibition show chassis (one for the Old World, one for the New) absorbed the five contracted frames. Meanwhile ERA continued with their

---

Reg Korner

Reg Korner was responsible for vehicle body design at Jowett from 1936 until the war interrupted car manufacture; he then worked on turning War Department designs into buildable products. On one occasion whilst wearing his Home Guard uniform (Home Guard duty was a once-weekly activity for Reg – one nervous night it fell to him to guard an unexploded bomb) he modelled for a photograph of a mortar Jowett was making. Soon after the Javelin project got under way he joined Palmer's small team. He liaised with Briggs, often travelling to Dagenham to sort out problems with the Javelin and also the Bradford van, and when the Jupiter project came along he designed the bodywork for that almost entirely himself.

Reg Korner, right, with Horace Grimley. (Woods Visual Imaging)

Reg was born in London in 1905, and grew up in Maida Vale. His parents ran a china shop in Oxford Street. After leaving Marylebone Grammar School at the age of fourteen, Reg learned the trade of body designer at the coachbuilding department of the Regent Street Polytechnic; he began his first job at the London Improved Coachbuilders in Pimlico, South London, then employing about 300 people. It was not to last. The end was accelerated for this particular company through the habit of the works manager and his assistant of organizing the construction of one or two cars above the number ordered in each contract, and quietly selling them off. So in 1926 Reg moved to Comptons at Hanwell; cars built there included four-seater tourer Bugattis at the rate of about one per week, as well as Bentley and Rolls-Royce – Comptons would exhibit their Jowett Arrow at Olympia in the early 1930s.

The 1930s were doubly tough for the coachbuilding industry, because in addition to the recession, all-steel bodywork was arriving and the days of coachbuilding were drawing to a close. After a number of other such jobs in the London area Reg realized the time had come to work for a real car firm, and so he moved to Coventry to Hillman/Humber, already part of the Rootes Group. The Rootes brothers had impractical ideas about car design and could not resist interfering: Reg made a tactical move to Austin just before the horror on which he had been working was quietly abandoned, with the sacking of some of the team: the proprietor, like the customer, is always right! He was soon to return to Hillman where he met Margaret his future wife. Reg was driving an MG at the time.

Around 1936, looking for a change of scenery, he wrote to Jowett on the off chance, suggesting that their cars were insufficiently curvy, and was taken on. From that date Jowetts became more stylish. Reg recalled that Willie Jowett was a retiring sort of fellow and of a peculiar shape: you got the seating right to his satisfaction, and then you had to change it to suit Mr Average!

When it became clear that the Javelin would not be ready for an early post-war launch, he and Palmer re-designed the 1938 commercial vehicle with the initial intention of producing 200 stop-gap vans, to be called the 'Bradford'. It fell to Reg to drive Bradford van no. 1 down to Briggs' Dagenham plant on VJ Day 1946, loaded with petrol in tins thanks to rationing and the rarity of filling stations then. On the journey he managed to turn it over, and although there was some spillage and a soaking for Reg, luckily there was no conflagration. Horace Grimley came to pick him up from hospital where a head-wound had needed stitches. Reg recalled that his Bradford-made woollen underwear smelled of petrol for weeks after that, but he lived to tell the tale and to contribute to the Javelin and Jupiter body designs.

After leaving Jowett – in somewhat unpleasant circumstances – Reg joined Morris Motors (soon to become BMC) where he updated the Minor. Later he worked on the front-drive projects, especially the Austin-Morris 1800, which with its legendary roadholding must be one of today's forgotten classics.

Reg was mild-mannered and sociable, although he did not make friends easily. He played golf, and liked a pint with friends in a pub. He found Yorkshire cold, which is why he was usually photographed wearing a hat. He was very good with his hands, and once did a complete loft conversion himself – even the design, construction and installation of the beautiful staircase was entirely his own work. Reg's Jupiter reflects his gentle but thorough-going personality as much as his sound eye for proportion and detail, qualities whose origins perhaps lie in his coachbuilding past. He died in 1992.

testing and completed their car, in that order, for the testing was done on a chassis supporting the crudest and most basic coachwork.

With the limited facilities at his disposal, there was only one way for Korner to succeed in his near-impossible task, and that was the body had to be constructed as a coachbuilder would tackle the work. Coachbuilders by definition design their coachwork to be right first time, because when a one-off car body is constructed for a customer there is little provision for development or second thoughts. Korner therefore dug deeply

into his coachbuilding experience. Tests showed that the chassis would flex – it had been ERA's intention to rely on FHC bodywork to provide stiffening – so Korner fitted a strong, steel bodyframe to the chassis with an element of flexibility built into its six mountings, which were essentially large, heavy-duty rubber bushes. Body panelling would be mounted onto the bodyframe and in this way, Korner hoped, the chassis could flex without disturbing the body structure. No matter that it would add weight.

Further, not only was the new car designed

The first Jowett 'Javelin-Jupiter' pictured on 30 March 1950. Only the two prototypes had that design of windscreen. (Woods Visual Imaging)

around coachbuilding techniques, an outside coachbuilder actually constructed the first two. This was King & Taylor of Godalming, Surrey, a large coachworks in those days – they employed about 100 people, and were building three coaches a fortnight in the early 1950s; today, a DIY superstore sits on the site that once employed highly skilled craftsmen. One of their projects was to build the special lorry that transported Campbell's Bluebird to its ill-fated world speed record attempt on Coniston Water. The company took in prototype work, and this included the Alvis Grey Lady and four Delahayes for various French motor shows. Another commission was to trim the body for Chitty Chitty Bang Bang.

Two chassis and bodyframes were sent down from Bradford. The bodywork was entirely fabricated in the panel shop from small pieces of flat aluminium sheet rolled and wheeled to fit wooden formers supplied by Jowett; they were then nibbled to final shape, and welded together. All these operations required great skill. The bonnet centre panel, for example, was made from about eighteen separate pieces, and the welds had to be ground down and planished to achieve a very

smooth finish with no hammer marks so that virtually no filler would be needed. The body was mounted on the chassis, the seats constructed (the seat looked like a bench seat but was in two halves, with the driver's side separately adjustable), the interiors trimmed, and the cars sent to Jowett in bare metal.

Progress was such that a press release could be issued on 31 January. Headed 'New Javelin model – the Jupiter', it went on: 'Jowett Cars Limited announce that good progress is being made with their new high performance car. It will be made at their Idle, Bradford, factory and will be known as the Jupiter…'. The name had apparently been suggested by Pomeroy, and a three-page article on the new car, presumably penned by Pomeroy, appeared in *The Motor* of 8 March.

By now there was only the single anti-roll bar, at the rear. The chassis had the tail extension, but was still constructed from only straight lengths of tube. Amongst the technical data the weight was given, very optimistically, as 13.5cwt (690kg), and the increased power of 60.5bhp, from what was outwardly the Javelin power unit, was supposed to come from a different camshaft and different carburettors – whereas in fact it came from different

Secure boot locker of the Mk 1 Jupiter, accessible only from inside the car. (LAT Photographic)

carburettors, exhaust manifolding and gas-flowed heads. The luggage space was said, also optimistically, to be 'very large', and it was mentioned that specially designed suitcases would be available; these 'Revelation cases' came to be listed in the spare parts book, but as far as is known they were not taken up in significant numbers, if at all. The article, which made no mention of Le Mans, concluded by stating that the Jupiter was not going to be marketed as a competition car, but 'it

Jupiter chassis at the 1951 Brussels Motor Show. Arthur Jopling is fifth from the left. (Le Maire)

is intended to fill the needs of those who seek a modern car that will combine high performance, comfort, roadworthiness and economy…'

The two prototypes were completed and running by the end of March 1950, a bare five months after Jowett took the decision to go it alone. As construction proceeded, drawings and templates were prepared so that further examples could be built either by King & Taylor or by Jowett. But there was a severe limit on the rate at which King & Taylor could produce body panels, forming them as they did by hand from flat sheet.

To supplement King & Taylor, Jowett implemented a new plan. This was to exhibit the show chassis aggressively at the main European motor shows, beginning with Brussels in mid-January 1950, with a view to getting Jupiters of differing styling constructed by outside coachbuilders. This was moderately successful, and orders began to come in for production chassis, with ultimately at least forty-two built in the UK, four handsome Jupiters by Stabilimenti Farina, six elegant

examples by three Swiss coachbuilders, and a quartet in Sweden, France, Holland and Denmark. In Australia a handful of bodies (some replica Jupiter) were fitted to rolling chassis.

Developments in 1950

1950 brought a very busy spring season to Grandfield and his men, because in addition to development of the Javelin and Bradford, there was now much Jupiter work to be done. Of the two prototypes, one was exhibition-prepared, road-tested one foggy Saturday over the Yorkshire moors, and shipped to New York for the British Automobile and Motor Cycle Show (15 to 23 April) for the official launch of the 'Javelin-Jupiter' – for that was now its name, and it was badged accordingly, as it was hoped it would help sell the Javelin. The Jowett stand had an exhibition chassis, a metallic grey LHD Javelin and the metallic bronze RHD Jupiter: the Hoffman Motor Car Company was signed up as the USA

Second prototype shown off in the Silverstone car park some time after its road test. Behind the Jupiter: Charles Grandfield (left) and Horace Grimley (centre). The rear-wing stoneguards are stainless steel. (Ted Miller collection)

Charles Grandfield

Charles Grandfield was a very important figure in the post-war history of Jowett. His experimental department was tasked with addressing all technical and reliability problems thrown up by the Javelin and Jupiter; with developing the Javelin, Jupiter and Bradford range; and with developing new models as well as specifying alternatives to hard-to-get components and materials – the 1940s and 1950s was a time of ongoing shortages and supply delays, where even the lack of a minor component could delay vehicle deliveries.

Charlie Grandfield.

Cyril 'Charlie' Grandfield was born in Chesterfield on 15 December 1914, and was educated at Chesterfield Grammar School. In 1931 he began a four-year apprenticeship at Austin, during which time he obtained his HNC in Automobile Engineering, with distinction. During this time he met Bert Hadley who was developing Austin competition cars and also driving them very rapidly. Grandfield worked in the Austin design office until joining Rolls Royce at Derby in 1939 on aero-engine design. Before the year was out he had entered the British army as a lieutenant, and served in several theatres of war; he also spent two years in Canada on tank training – he considered that his exposure to the clear sunlight in this country caused his (cured) skin cancer that developed much later. He was three times mentioned in dispatches, and was promoted to major, and then to lieutenant colonel in 1943. He was demobilized in 1946, and joined Sir Roy Fedden as works director developing a flat-six sleeve-valve aero engine and a 1300hp gas turbine. He joined Jowett in 1948 as engineering manager.

Grandfield had a good war, rising to managing Montgomery's transport during the final push across Europe, and he was decorated by the Dutch government. But those who knew him before and after the conflict said that the war changed him: many found him arrogant. Perhaps it was this streak of arrogance that enabled him fearlessly to take Jowett into top flight international racing and rallying, once the ice had been broken. It should be remembered that the 1949 Monte Carlo class winner was a private entrant, and for the Spa event the entrance fee was paid by ERA.

Grandfield built up the experimental department from being little more than Horace Grimley and some bench-testing equipment, to a thriving section of more than twenty people. He was generally liked and respected by his subordinates as firm but fair and a good leader; but he and Grimley had their disagreements on technical matters, Grimley being extremely experienced and resourceful – there were times when it was not easy for him. The problems thrown up by the post-war cars were many and varied, both in terms of development and the design of new products, as well as the competition programme. In fact there was no competition department as such, and everything had to be fitted into the experimental department's programme and budget. Grandfield was the chef d'équipe, and it was thanks to his commitment, energy and determination that the factory cars were as successful as they were – no mean achievement for Grandfield, his team, and a limited budget.

Grandfield was determined to secure the future of the company by attracting new, young engineers to Jowett. To this end he offered post-graduate training for newly qualified automobile and mechanical engineers, two in 1951 and two in 1952. However, his star began to wane during the latter year, and he left Jowett in 1953.

Known by some as Charlie Cornfield and by others as Granny, Grandfield had quarrelled with Bert Hadley, who combined the talents of being one of the quickest racing drivers of his time with technical excellence in the automotive field. It required an impassioned plea from Jopling to bring Hadley back into the fold. Hadley felt he had much to offer Jowett in terms of engineering expertise and results as a driver, but Grandfield (perhaps deliberately, perhaps not) provided him with poorly prepared cars on two occasions; given good preparation (the 1951 RAC-TT) Hadley delivered the goods. In another example of a wasted talent, after Bill Robinson's superb performance on the Monaco GP circuit at the end of the 1951 Monte Carlo Rally, Grandfield offered him a works Le Mans drive – only to abruptly withdraw the offer when Marcel Becquart appeared on the scene.

Grandfield died in 1998.

representative, and others would follow. Hoffman also sold Aston Martin and Porsche at that time.

It was as if, perhaps from some ancient mythology, the Jupiter had three parents. Palmer provided the drive train and suspension, Eberhorst the chassis, and Korner the bodywork. In Korner's long career in the motor industry, the Jupiter was the only car for which he designed the coachwork wholly himself, and his love for the curve was given full rein. Grandfield's role was to be the Jupiter's midwife, and he threw himself enthusiastically into the task. In his long career in the motor industry it was the only car that he would bring into this world alive and kicking.

The second prototype was registered GKU 764, and the remainder of March 1950 was spent sorting, evaluating, road-testing and in development work. On 6 April its continental road-test run began, the car being crewed by Charles Grandfield and Horace Grimley. On 9 April they arrived at Le Mans and spent the night there. The next morning they investigated the circuit and concluded the necessary negotiations for accommodation at the Hôtel Moderne (where the famous Bentley teams stayed) for the race period. A number of circuits of the course (still all public roads then) was made before leaving for Cahors, which they reached late that evening after covering the 348 miles (560km) at the rapid average speed of 54mph (87km/h). The car was back at base on 14 April, having covered 2,888 miles (4,647km) at a running average of over 46mph (74km/h) for the nine days; this means that it must have been held close to its maximum speed of just over 90mph (145km/h) for quite a lot of the driving time. The crew came back with many recommendations that were implemented on production models, and an immediate sanction for twenty-five cars was put through.

Meanwhile work was proceeding on the race car, a very much simpler and lighter version of the two prototypes. It was completed about mid-April and registered GKW 111, perhaps the most famous registration mark to adorn a Jowett: it was being readied to race as the 'Javelin Jupiter'.

The Jupiter Takes Off

Following its launch, the message that came back from New York was that Jupiters were needed by the score, or maybe even by the hundred, and this was reinforced a month later when the Javelin-Jupiter romped home at Le Mans. Jowett was now presented with a serious manufacturing problem: how to make Jupiter body panels in quantity. Briggs were approached, but were not interested. The problem was solved by Arthur Jopling, Jowett's managing director, who was also on the board of Miles Aircraft, a company noted for its trainer aircraft. Miles had rubber-bed presses that were used for forming aircraft wing and fuselage panels, and could be used for low-volume car panels. Some low-cost tooling was required, and when this was in place, body parts became available in far larger quantities than King & Taylor could aspire to. The bonnet centre panel was now made from three instead of eighteen separate pieces, and the large and complex tail panel was made from only two pressings. The shapes were approximate, still needing extensive panel-beating, rolling and welding skills to achieve an acceptable standard for what was a high-priced luxury car for the time.

After the two prototypes it is believed King & Taylor made a further ten or so body sets in two or perhaps three batches, for delivery to Bradford for final assembly. Jowett completed the first five standard Jupiters by September 1950 approximately, and the second about nine weeks later. It is not known if King & Taylor made the panelling for the 1950 Le Mans contender, but it is highly probable. Thanks to Miles' rubber-bed presses, the output of standard cars climbed to a maximum of eighty per month during the third quarter of 1951, with another peak of thirty per month in the beginning of 1953.

The Korner-designed heavier body meant that the front and rear suspension torsion-rod springs could be the same as the Javelin's, and the remaining anti-roll bar was deleted possibly because no one at Jowett understood anti-roll bars or how to select their spring rates. The heavier body and lack of body stiffening of the overall structure meant

Unusual bonnet lifting arrangement. Spring-tensioned telescopic struts support the heavy bonnet. (Woods Visual Imaging)

that the chassis had to be strengthened, and all Jupiter chassis have lengths of angle-iron welded to the underside of the main chassis side-members.

A curiosity inherited from the original ERA design, and which survived for several hundred Jupiters, was the chassis-mounted oil cooler just ahead of the radiator: as with the Javelin, the Jupiter's water radiator is behind the engine. Depending upon the amount of heat rejected by the oil cooler, there would be the possibility of

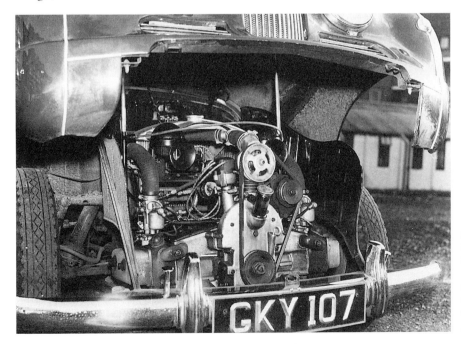

Good accessibility is provided to the engine, although radiator replenishment is a knack. The finned chassis-mounted oil cooler can just be made out to the right of the offside carburettor. (LAT Photographic)

the water radiator being cooled by hot air, an inconvenience corrected when this oil-cooler type was deleted, following reports of oil leakage from it. Another curiosity in the early Jupiters was the carburettor air intakes just behind the radiator. This had two effects: first, the hotter rather than cooler air entering the engine would reduce volumetric efficiency, hence maximum power output; and second, radiator cooling would be assisted, as at 70mph the engine would be gulping air at about 40 litres per second, which would have helped the cooling system, somewhat on the marginal side for the Jupiter. In the search for more power, this feature was deleted in later cars, and replaced by individual pancake air-cleaners above the carburettors.

Jupiters were not always delivered in serial number order – for example, chassis 656, 678, 679, 705, 708, 712, 720, 733, 747, 755 should have left the factory in March or April 1952 when they were constructed, but in fact were shipped

Well-restored Jupiter engine bay, bonnet removed. Late pancake air filters and late rubber-bushed front suspension can be seen. (Ron Leech)

Cockpit controls. This early Jupiter has a Javelin throttle pedal; later Jupiters had an improved version providing easier heel-and-toe. (LAT Photographic)

A Jupiter Road Test

This subjective test drive of the Jupiter was published in *Cheshire Life – Yorkshire Illustrated* of May 1953. The author, using the pen-name Phaeton, wrote:

After a hard day's work in London I might have been considered crazy to test a motor car on a run to Manchester by night, particularly as I had a reserved seat on the evening 'plane. I arrived at Messrs Jowett's London headquarters feeling jaded, and disinclined to drive two hundred miles. By the time I had stowed my bags away in the [Mk1a Jupiter's] boot, drunk some tea, and prepared myself for a long fast run, the offices of London had opened their doors to allow several millions of people to return to their homes, and the streets were crowded. However, before I had threaded my way across Piccadilly in the open Jupiter I was as stimulated as if I had come into a fortune.

The Jupiter being a comparatively small car I was able to thread my way through the traffic without much difficulty. Despite a performance that turned the natural handicap of London into an even chance with the taxi-driver, it took me half an hour to cover the first seven miles. However, as it grew dark the traffic thinned and I increased speed. I raised the hood, which is neatly stowed beneath a waterproof cover, in thirty seconds; only two screws are required to fix this firmly, and with the windows wound up there was the snugness of a saloon.

As I made my way north along the A5 I learned more about this amazing small car. It is difficult to believe that the engine is only 1,500cc, for it has a greater flexibility than I could have imagined, though to get the sparkling performance that it provides, the gearbox must be used constantly. Seventy is obtainable in third gear, and the car corners with precision. I took it around corners in power slides and at speeds that would have been too fast for nearly any car I know, but without any feeling of instability. My top speed shown on the speedometer was over 90mph at about 5,500rpm – but the great feature of this journey on a road with a high proportion of bends and few long straight stretches was the high average speed without fuss. Anywhere between 70mph and 80mph is the cruising speed, and my running time for this journey was four hours for 197 miles, of which the first seven took half an hour – a very high average for safe motoring on British roads.

The steering is excellent, very direct and sensitive, but without road bumps being transmitted back to the driver. In fact, on the roughest surfaces there was little need to throttle back, for the springing is such that no discomfort is felt. The bodywork has the elegance that one expects to see more often in Italian and French cars than British: the lines are those of a thoroughbred, and the car always caused comment, I found, wherever parked.

London, a summer's day in 1951. A chance meeting of two Jowett owners. (Collection Joves)

between May and October 1953, and had some, but not all modifications appropriate to cars built from scratch at that later time. By contrast, although Mk1a series production begins in October 1952 at chassis 940, most of the Mk1 Jupiters built significantly after that date – for instance, E3 SA 866R completed 22 May 1953 – carried all the latest modifications. In other words, it is sometimes the date and sometimes the chassis number or body number that is important.

Every panel of each bodyset was numbered as a manufacturing and assembly aid – since the bonnet was made from three pressings, the body number appears on it in three places. This reminds us that the working and trimming of the original panel pieces took place in a different workshop from the welding of the pieces together, and the finishing. The body panels being unique to each car were not easily interchangeable. The first production Jupiter, chassis 17, has body set 1; because of this, and because some chassis were delivered naked to coachbuilders, and because some chassis numbers were never actually issued at all, the body number of a standard Mk1 Jupiter is always lower than the chassis number, and sometimes much lower: for example, chassis 876 has bodyset number 664. The last Mk1 to find a customer was chassis 936, body number 725, which went to

Henfield, Sussex on 30 October 1953. Somewhat confusingly, the highest Mk1 chassis number was 939, this car being shipped to Japan on 10 September 1952. For the Jupiter, chassis numbering and car completion was not a well co-ordinated procedure at Jowett! Body numbering began again at 1 for the Mk1a.

Details of Body Design – Mark 1

A number of visual bodywork changes was made during the production life of the Mk1 Jupiter. What follows is intended as a guide to body development, rather than an exhaustive pointer to details that any individual Mk1 Jupiter should or should not possess. Jupiter assembly was a lengthy and at times relatively haphazard activity, and changes were rarely made at a defined chassis number. Javelin and Bradford assembly would normally take precedence, and it is also possible that export Jupiters took precedence over cars for the home market.

One short-lived but very obvious feature appearing on the early Jupiter is the fore and aft strakes. These are separate, shaped aluminium mouldings which, though appearing formed in the panels, are in fact bolted onto the front and rear wings. Strakes appeared only on the two

Early Jupiter showing its unlouvred bonnet. This picture must have been taken in late November or early December 1950. (Ted Miller collection)

prototypes, the first Le Mans car (GKW 111) in its post-Le Mans guise, and the first five production Jupiters – from which the 1951 Monte Carlo Rally three-car works team was drawn. The prototype of the Mk1a had strakes of a different form, but only at the front.

The deletion of the strakes did not immediately coincide with a change to the shape of a return formed in the front wings (see photos below). Although not hard and fast to a chassis number, this changeover seems to have begun with Jupiters delivered around the end of August 1951, and to

Jupiter Changes

Front wing detail was initially not tapered (left), as required for the strakes. Around July 1951 this detail became tapered (right).

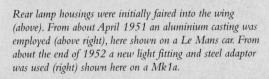

Rear lamp housings were initially faired into the wing (above). From about April 1951 an aluminium casting was employed (above right), here shown on a Le Mans car. From about the end of 1952 a new light fitting and steel adaptor was used (right) shown here on a Mk1a.

Jupiter Changes (*cont.*)

Early Jupiters had Javelin-Jupiter bonnet emblems (inserts shown above) to reflect its original name. Some time in 1951 this changed to Jowett Jupiter (right).

Initially Jupiter bonnets were unlouvred. From about June 1951 two plates of four louvres were bolted in (left). At or some time after November 1951 louvres were formed into the bonnet in two groups of seven (right).

Stone guards on rear wings were initially metal (left), here aluminium. After about May 1952 these tended to become moulded rubber (right) shown here on a Mk1a.

have become standardized by chassis 400. A similar, but rather less noticeable change was made to the rear wings at about the same time.

In February 1951 the factory announced that the Javelin-Jupiter was henceforth to be called the Jowett Jupiter, requiring a change to the bonnet badge (see photos on page 64). This didn't stop the factory from continuing to fit Javelin-Jupiter badges until supplies of the new emblem were assured (probably some time before 1951 was out) and even then, perhaps to use up old stock, some 1953 Jupiters were delivered with Javelin-Jupiter badges.

Initially the rear lamp housings were neatly faired into the rear wings and tail panel (see page 63). The change to separate aluminium castings is believed to have coincided with the construction of the first batch of Californian Jupiters, starting with chassis 122 and delivered in late April 1951. From about February or March 1952, for those chassis somewhere in the 600s, a pressed-steel housing was introduced, similar to that used on the Javelin and requiring a different lamp unit.

Early Jupiter bonnets were unlouvred, as can be seen from some of the photographs in this book. From August 1951, at about chassis 190, two separate four-louvre panels were screw-fitted as standard. This change seems to have been brought in because it offered a functional advantage – the reduction of a tendency towards overheating in slowly moving or stationary traffic – and as usual there was no exact introduction point. It is even possible there was a disagreement at the factory, suggested by Jupiter 165 whose bonnet was cut for louvre plates, but the holes then welded up! Louvre panels for retrofitting to unlouvred bonnets were available on request, and there are known instances of non-factory louvres added in the field. Some Jupiters still exist with unlouvred bonnets. A few Jupiters were built with two separate, screw-fitted, seven-louvre panels. The changeover to two groups of seven louvres formed directly and more neatly into the bonnet centre panel was, as usual, not hard and fast to a chassis number, and gradually appeared in the 400s to become standardized by about chassis number 490 in December 1951.

The rear wing stoneguards started out as metal (see photo page 64), initially stainless steel then subsequently aluminium. The change of metals may have taken place around August 1951, coinciding with the alterations to the wings noted above. From about chassis 800 around the end of April 1952 the stoneguards became black rubber mouldings as for the Mk1a. At about the same time, the previously fitted wooden door cappings gave way to painted aluminium ones, again as for the Mk1a.

One change that came and went almost unremarked during 1952 was to the headlamp rims: instead of being chrome-plated, they might be painted the colour of the car. A study of period photographs indicates that quite some Jupiters completed in the first quarter of 1952 have this feature, which subtly alters the look of the car from the front.

California-specification Jupiters were all left-hand drive, had flasher turn indicators (initially trafficator slots were plated over, later they were deleted) and locally produced and fitted sealed beam headlamp inserts.

The Mark 1a

The Mk1a was introduced in October 1952, but the Mk1 continued to be available until October 1953 at a slightly reduced price. The very last Mk1a (of course, also the very last Jowett-built vehicle) to leave the factory went to a Bradford customer on 4 November 1954.

The Mk1a remained unchanged for its two-year production life, with ninety-four examples constructed. The thinking behind this model was not to develop it as a competition car, but rather to provide an externally-accessible luggage compartment, to alter the hood line to be more modern and rakish, and to introduce some cost-cutting changes such as the symmetrical metal instrument panel, now almost the same whatever the hand of drive. The chassis was altered at the rear, and simplified, to provide space for the larger boot, and the bodyframe was more firmly located to the chassis by cross-bracing between the chassis front structure and

Jupiter Models, 1950–54

General:

Drophead coachwork. Aluminium panels on steel body-frame assembly fitted to tubular steel chassis, folding hood. Leather-upholstered bench seat, width 44in (111.8cm). Detachable Triplex safety glass windscreen, replaceable by aeroscreens for competition, and winding glass side windows. Mk1 has a luggage locker in the tail accessible from behind the seat; Mk1a has a boot opening from the outside, made possible by chassis and body-frame alterations at the rear.

Production life with delivery dates:

Jupiter Mk1 (SA) model March 1950 to November 1953, largely for export until October 1951.
Jupiter Mk1a (SC) went into production from October 1952, and then the Mk1 was confined to the home market, apart from a couple of exports and a handful of personal export cars, Mk1a (chassis 560 and 940 onwards) October 1952 to November 1954. Both models available in rolling chassis form for specialist coachwork, with the last chassis shipped in March 1952 save for the one only Mk1a chassis; this was sent to Beirut in March 1953 and never heard from again.

Total number of cars built:

731 Mk1 and 94 Mk1a standard body cars, and 75 rolling chassis. Almost but not quite all the rolling chassis were built into completed cars.

Engine:

Four-cylinder, horizontally opposed overhead valve. Die-cast aluminium two-piece cylinder block with cast-iron wet liners.
Crankshaft mounted in steel-back shell bearings, front and centre copper/lead/indium, rear white metal with integral thrust faces.
Valves pushrod-operated from central cast-iron camshaft. Zero-lash hydraulic tappets on a few early cars, later replaced with solid versions.
Twin Zenith carburettors.
SU electric fuel pump.
Pressure-fed lubrication from sump-mounted oil pump driven by worm gear on crankshaft.
Coil and contact breaker ignition.
Cooling by pressurized water system with belt-driven water pump incorporating cooling fan on extension shaft.
Water radiator mounted to rear of engine. Oil cooler optional.
Crankcase breather recirculatory.

Engine dimensions and capacities:

Bore and stroke: 72.5 × 90mm.
Swept volume: 1,486cc.
Compression ratio: 7.6, or 8.0:1 on some export models.
Output: 60bhp at 4,750rpm (January 1952) raised to 62.5bhp at 4,500rpm (January 1953).
Oil cooler: Chassis-mounted finned tube from start. From 1952 engine-mounted type fitted when available (usually for export).
Fuel capacity: Mk1 = 10 gallons (45 litres), Mk1a = 8 gallons (36 litres).

Clutch:

Borg & Beck 7.25in single dry plate.

Gearbox:

Four forward ratios plus reverse. Constant load synchromesh on second, third and top. Higher-geared intermediate ratios fitted virtually from start of production. Steering column gearchange.

Dimensions:

Wheelbase: 93in (2,362mm)
Track: 52in (1,321mm) front, 50.5in (1,283mm) rear
Overall length: 168in (4,268mm)
Overall width: 62in (1,575mm)
Kerb weight: 2,100lb (955)kg

Chassis construction:

Welded chromium molybdenum tubular steel, 3in (76mm) diameter 16swg for main side members, and 2in (51mm) diameter 18swg for struts and torsional stiffness members.

Steering:

Straight rack and pinion, 2³/₄ turns lock to lock, average turning circle 31ft 6in (9.6m).

Front suspension:

Independent, unequal length parallel wishbone with longitudinal torsion bars. Metal bushed front suspension from outset, rubber bushed from late 1952.
Telescopic shock absorbers.

Rear suspension:

Four parallel trailing arms with transverse torsion bars. Panhard rod located from axle bracket. Telescopic shock absorbers. Live axle with Salisbury hypoid bevel. Final drive ratio 4.1:1 (some 1950 Jupiters only), all other Jupiters 4.56:1 providing 16.9mph (27.3km/h) per 1,000rpm in top gear.

Wheels:

Pressed steel ventilated disc 3-16in, tyre size 5.50-16in cross-ply.

Brakes:

Girling hydro-mechanical. Cast-iron hub/drum assemblies 9in (229mm) diameter. Single-leading, single trailing shoes width 1.5in (38mm). Front hydraulically operated, rear width 1.25in (31.75mm) mechanically operated by rod from master cylinder. Changed to full hydraulic January 1951 approximately at chassis 56.

Electrics:

Two 6-volt batteries in series mounted behind the seat (Mk1), single 12-volt battery (Mk1a).
Twelve-volt headlamps double-dip, Lucas PF770 MkII flat lens (except California Jupiters which had local-standard sealed beam headlamp inserts fitted on arrival).

Turn indicators:

Semaphore arms except California, for which an interrupter flasher system was fitted.

Instruments:

Speedometer and mechanical tachometer 5in (127mm) diameter; clock in speedometer. Engine oil pressure and temperature, water temperature, ammeter, and fuel in four 2in- (51mm) diameter gauges; instruments set behind walnut veneer fascia (Mk1) with similar chrome-bezel instruments mounted on painted metal fascia (Mk1a).

Extras:

Radio, heater, rimbellishers.

Performance:

Mk1: 0–60mph (97km/h) in 14.2sec, standing ¹/₄ mile in 21.0sec, max speed 88mph (141.5km/h), consumption 23mpg (12.3ltr/100km) (*Autosport* January 1952).
Mk1a:. 0–60mph in 16.8sec, standing ¹/₄ mile in 20.7sec, 40–60mph in 9.0sec (third), 12.0sec (top). Max speed 84.2mph (135.4km/h), consumption 21.8mpg (13ltr/100km). Fuel 80-octane. (*The Autocar* January 1953)

This hardtop, made from aluminium over ash, was commercially available from a London coachbuilder. (Charles Dunn)

Prototype Mk1a showing strake, symmetrical instrument panel and mid-period rear lamp housing. (Woods Visual Imaging)

bodyframe, combined with firmer front body to chassis mounts. Examples of the Mk1 built after the introduction of the Mk1a also had this modification, and a retro kit was available for existing Mk1 Jupiters. This obviated problems of scuttle shake and occasional door sticking.

The externally opening boot has a larger capacity than the internal luggage locker of the Mk1, and the raked hood and associated cockpit changes allow more space for the internal carriage of smaller items; the company claimed that it was now possible for the Jupiter to carry not only two people but their personal effects 'for a long tour', thus addressing an oft-repeated and not entirely unfair criticism. The enlarged boot required amongst other changes the relocation of the petrol tank, and one result of this was the provision of slightly less leg room for the larger driver, with some customers significantly taller than 6 foot preferring the Mk1 model.

The Mk1a has these visually distinguishing features compared with the Mk1:

Windscreen glasses have no chrome surrounds.

Instrument panel is metal (painted the colour of the body) rather than wood, and instruments are clustered symmetrically around the car's centreline rather than in front of the driver.

Door cappings are painted aluminium (as for the later Mk1) rather than wood.

Hood is raked further back compared with the Mk1.

External opening to the boot with visible hinges and operating handle.

Fuel filler cap now on the right side of the body relocated to a more forward, higher position between boot lid and waist rail.

Prototype Mk1a showing raked hoodline and cavernous boot. (Woods Visual Imaging)

The Jupiter can seat three. (Collection Joves)

Jupiter Sales Pitch

The Jupiter had considerable pretensions to luxury and was priced accordingly. In September 1951, the UK retail price (basic price) of the Jupiter was £1,394 (£895), the same as the 1,500cc HRG, but nearly twice the price of the MG Midget at £733 (£470), with the Morgan Plus 4 Drophead Coupé at £880 (£565). Higher priced sports cars were the XK120 at £1,678 (£1,078), the Healey Abbott Drophead at £2,335 (£1,500) and the Aston Martin DB2 Drophead at £2,879 (£1,850). But in contrast to its cheaper rivals the Jupiter offered modern, eye-catching Italian-derived styling, a soft ride, light steering, accurate roadholding with little body roll, glass wind-up windows, a lined mohair hood quick to erect and lower, and providing snug coupé comfort, a comfortable leather-trimmed bench seat that could accommodate three at a pinch (gear-

changing was by Javelin-derived column shift), cruising speeds up to 90mph (145km/h) and a range of up to 250 miles (400km) on a tankful. The walnut-faced instrument panel was populated with a large rev counter (redbanded at 5,500–6,000rpm) and speedometer whose maximum mark was perhaps optimistic at 120mph (193km/h). The choice of three metallic and at least four non-metallic paint colours was offered, with two upholstery colours.

This, then, was the Jowett Jupiter: a racing pedigree and a luxury coachbuilt drophead coupé body, offered by a company with little sporting heritage apart from the Javelin's dramatic international rally win at Monte Carlo, and even more dramatic race win at Spa.

Early successes lead to great expectations, and these are hard to live up to. Later chapters explore how the Jupiter fared in the big time.

Specification and Price by Year

Prices are UK retail price (basic, or pre-tax price). Colours are as stated in the Jowett brochures and factory records.

1950 Colours – Metallic copper, metallic turquoise blue, British racing green, scarlet (Italian red). beige upholstery and fawn hood. September prices: chassis £671.58 (£525), Mk1 car £1,086.87 (£850).

1951 Colours – Metallic copper, Metallic turquoise blue, British racing green, scarlet (Italian red), ivory. beige or red upholstery and fawn hood (except ivory body colour, which was trimmed with black hood and red interior only). Prices: chassis £690.75 (540), Mk1 car £1,393.72 (£895). Optional HMV radiomobile fitted at £49.50 including tax. From April, LHD model FOB New York $2,850.

1952 Colours – Metallic copper, metallic turquoise blue, metallic Connaught green, British racing green, scarlet (Italian red), ivory. beige or red upholstery and fawn hood (ivory body colour, trimmed as for 1951). January prices: chassis unchanged from 1951. Mk1 car £1,518.17 (£975). August prices: Mk1 car £1,284.93 (£825). October prices: Mk1 car as before, Mk1a £1,393.72 (£895). Chassis no longer listed, although three chassis were delivered in March with one later returned to the factory and assembled into a Jupiter during August.

1953 Colours – Mk1 and Mk1a: Metallic copper, metallic turquoise blue, metallic Connaught green, British racing green, scarlet (Italian red), ivory, bottle green. beige or red upholstery and fawn hood (ivory body colour, trimmed as for 1951). May price for the Mk1a: £1,127.50 (£795). October price: £1,028.21 (£725). Ash-framed aluminium hardtop offered at £130 by Wm Park (Coachbuilders) Ltd of Kew, London. List price in the USA $3,295.

1954 Colours – Mk1a only: Metallic turquoise blue, scarlet (Italian red), ivory, bottle green. beige or red upholstery and fawn hood (Ivory body colour, trimmed as for 1951). Price unchanged from 1953.

6 The Fixed-Head Coupé Jupiter

Jowett produced only series production Jupiters, excepting the three racing R1s and the three R4 prototypes. All Jupiters with non-standard bodies were constructed by independent coachbuilders – even the professionally made hardtops found on Jupiters in the USA, the UK and Australia were private ventures, and such units were never available from the factory.

The specially prepared show chassis was exhibited at London, Paris, Brussels, Turin, Amsterdam, Geneva and Zurich, and another appeared at New York and Pasadena California. This marketing exercise resulted in over three-score special-bodied Jupiters being constructed – some by the most celebrated coachbuilders of the day – at a time when there still existed a coachbuilding tradition

in the motor industry. Almost half were fitted with saloon, or fixed-head coupé bodywork.

Rolling chassis were supplied very fully equipped. They could be, and indeed were, sometimes driven. All the instruments were supplied, also the electrics including lights, switches and wiring harness, and sometimes bumpers and grilles. Coachwork was supposed to be approved by Jowett, and a grille pattern approximately resembling the standard car was requested. This was generally adhered to, either exactly with the supplied standard grille set, or something that alluded to it. A very few constructors ignored this request. Normally the then-current Jupiter bonnet emblem would be fitted. The coachbuilt Jupiter was accepted by the factory as a Jowett,

Hardtop offered by Angell Motors of Pasadena. Weight 21lb (9.5kg). It takes three minutes to fit leaving the folded hood in place. (Ted Miller collection)

and covered by the normal six-month guarantee from the date of delivery to the customer.

The Italian Influence

Initially the intention was to rely on the independents for a significant proportion of Jupiter production. One of the most celebrated coachbuilders of the day was Stabilmenti Farina of via Tortona, Turin, then loosely associated with the more famous Pininfarina; Stabilmenti Farina was in fact founded by Pinin's father.

Leslie Johnson had involved Farina from the outset, during the ERA period late in 1949, and Farina were given a drawing of the ERA version of the frame. However, the first actual Farina Jupiter, of dazzling beauty and originality for the time, was constructed on the second production chassis to the order of Jowett. The car was built swiftly and with great skill and intelligence, with no more than sixty days between the chassis assembly leaving the factory and the completed car appearing, fully finished, at the Paris Salon of 6 October 1950; it resembles somewhat the Lancia Aurelia B20 of the period. This Jupiter is essentially a strong steel shell welded to the chassis, with additional support structure.

London's Earls Court Motor Show, October 1949. Jupiter exhibition chassis as designed and built by ERA Ltd. (Collection Joves)

Jupiter by J. J. Armstrong of Carlisle, finished in dark maroon with blue leather upholstery; the instrument panel was walnut. The car was not registered until July 1952, but it is known to have run earlier on trade plates. (From a drawing by Malcolm Bergin)

The Farina split the Jowett top brass, few of whom were aware of the extraordinary creativity of the emerging post-war Italian coachbuilding industry. 'We don't want that foreign muck!' was

the famous and baffling management response to what could have been a world beater. As a result only four in all were constructed, all surviving to the present. But the Farina Jupiter inspired another two similar cars that were commissioned from the British coachbuilder Coachcraft of Egham; one went racing at Goodwood (where it won) in the hands of its then owner, a test pilot with the Miles Aircraft Company. At the time of writing this car is owned by the former World Champion on both two wheels and four, John Surtees – indeed this is not his first Jupiter, because he began four-wheel motoring with a standard Mk1 Jupiter in the mid-1950s.

These Coachcraft Jupiters, as well as the Adams & Robinson, the Epsom Motor Panels and one or two other saloon Jupiters, were constructed around the then-revolutionary Superleggera (super-light) principle pioneered by the Italian coachworks Touring of Milan. A superstructure of small-bore steel tubing was welded to the chassis, over which was formed the aluminium panelling. All these Jupiters were strongly influenced by contemporary Italian coupé styling.

Marcel Becquart's Farina (the third such car) visiting Le Mans in 1952. (Ferret Fotographics)

First Coachcraft Jupiter, shown here in the early 1960s wearing later registration. (Collection Joves)

Coachcraft Jupiter's engine bay is more accessible than it looks, for the large grille is easily removed. (Collection Joves)

Saloon Jupiters for Racing and Rallying

By the London Motor Show of October 1951, when Jupiter manufacture was in full swing at Bradford and at last the Jupiter became available on the home market, 37 per cent of units delivered at that time had been chassis. Prior to that show, few of the British public could buy the standard product, and had to make do with a coachbuilder's variant. Bill Robinson, fresh from his triumph in the 1951 Monte in a works Jupiter – where he took the class, thanks to some very

The Jupiter of Bill Robinson is prepared for the British Empire Trophy race, Isle of Man, 14 June 1951, from which it retired on lap 11. (Collection Joves)

This KW-bodied Jupiter was raced by Albert Wake at Aintree in 1954. (Collection Joves)

J. F. Hall racing a KW Jupiter at Snetterton on 13 August 1955. (Charles Dunn)

fast and accurate driving round the Monaco Grand Prix circuit – had to have a saloon Jupiter built for him in order to race. This event, another at Goodwood, and one or two more (J. F. Hall raced one at Snetterton as late as August 1955) underscored the fact that the saloon Jupiter's forte was not racing, but rallying.

The coachbuilder Ghia of Aigle, Switzerland, which had a very faint, shadowy connection with the better known eponymous Turin factory, constructed two saloon Jupiters. One was entered in two rallies but failed to start in either, as it turned out, not being ready in time for the first and not running satisfactorily for the second. Although one of these handsome machines is apparently lost to us, the other survives in a small French collection near Bergerac and deserves to be restored. All the other Swiss-built Jupiters – including the award-winner by Gebruder Beutler and another by Ghia Aigle – were dropheads. Beutler is probably best known for building under contract the Porsche 356 Speedster between 1954 and 1958.

The 1952 rule change for the Monte Carlo Rally allowing only closed cars – which could, however, be coachbuilt variants on standard series-production open-car chassis – meant that a number of saloon Jupiters (and indeed saloon variants of other open cars) came to be built for this most famous of all international rallies. In competition terms Marcel Becquart's Farina was the most successful of these Jupiters, as it came close to outright victory in 1952.

The Lancashire coachbuilder J. E. Farr of Blackburn constructed a saloon Jupiter for Robert Ellison to drive in the 1952 Monte. Interior equipment included bucket seats (essential for the navigator during high-speed driving whilst map-reading or timing), and on the passenger side, an extra horn button, a sliding map tray with lamp fitted below the instrument panel glove locker, and a small detachable panel for twin stopwatches.

Alas the stopwatches never went into action, because this particular Monte was hit by extremely severe winter weather, and the Farr was one of the many casualties along the final run-in to Monaco. Ambitiously, the company followed with three more examples, of which just one is known for sure to have been scrapped. The Monte Carlo Farr survives in excellent order.

From the middle of 1952, factory Jupiter panels became available. Frank Grounds, the Birmingham

The ash-framed Farr Jupiter prepared for the 1952 Monte Carlo Rally. The bonnet, with in-built Marchal fog and spotlights, was designed for good engine accessibility. Turn indication was by flashers, tankage for 20 gallons was provided, and the spare wheel locker could take two wheels with snow chains. (Collection Joves)

The Jupiter of Frank Grounds, here driven by Mrs Lola Grounds in the 1953 International RAC Rally of Great Britain. (Brymer)

P. Gay drives Jean Latune's French-bodied Jupiter in the 1953 Charbo. (Collection Joves)

Jaguar and Jowett agent, used the standard bonnet cleverly mated to a close-couple four-seater saloon body designed and con-structed in his own coachbuilding facility. In the 1953 Monte, following the elimination of Becquart, Frank moved up to class fourth, while the French-built saloon Jupiter of Jean Latune, president of the Auto Club de la Drôme, came two places lower. Both these Jupiters engaged in a number of events in their own countries, providing as they did excellent rally vehicles for those times. The Grounds Jupiter took part in the RAC and Scottish RAC rallies of 1953, as well as events local to Birmingham, while Latune competed in two Tour de France d'Automobile, two Montes, and a Charbo (Lyon–Charbonnières).

British Coachbuilders

Some owners just wanted to look smart and cut a dash in an all-weather Jupiter, and these customers found that a saloon model sounded like a Jupiter, felt like a Jupiter, and went and handled like a Jupiter, but had the comfort and convenience of a fixed-head coupé.

One of the best-known of British coachbuilders of the time was Abbott of Farnham. Abbott built two open and two closed Jupiters, with one open and one closed going in for competition, though in a very limited way. The Flewitt company, a small Birmingham coachworks better known for its Rolls-Royce, Daimler and Austin bodywork, constructed a Jupiter, using, like Frank Grounds, a standard Jupiter front end; but perhaps the most aesthetically successful of such creations has to be the Danish-built Jupiter by Sommer of Copenhagen. This happens to be the only left-hand-drive special-bodied Jupiter; in styling it resembles a Bentley Continental in miniature.

The saloon body fitted to chassis 12 by J. J. Armstrong of Carlisle used the traditional ash wood-framing with aluminium panelling. This was a working car up to 1968, but then had to endure three decades of serious neglect. At the time of writing it is being carefully and thoroughly restored.

Abbott of Farnham fitted this body to a Jupiter chassis in January 1952 for a Halifax customer. Another Abbott saloon and two dropheads still survive. (The Autocar)

The Danish-built Sommer Jupiter, the only left-hand-drive example, is alive and well living in its homeland. (Collection Joves)

Armstrong Jupiter as found.
(S. Wood)

Interior of the Jupiter, as rescued.
(S. Wood)

About fourteen fixed-head coupé Jupiters survive to this day, all stylistically varied, all interesting in their way, and many in running order or under restoration. This number includes three Monte Carlo participants: Becquart's Farina, Grounds' saloon, and the Farr of Robert Ellison, not forgetting the Adams & Robinson saloon built for the 1953 Monte but not finished in time.

Restoration under way, as the new ash frame receives the recovered aluminium panelling. (S. Wood)

Amstrong's body restoration nearly complete! (S. Wood)

Gomm-bodied Jupiter first saw the open road in 1960 (Collection Joves)

A few Jupiter rolling chassis were returned to the factory and built into standard Jupiters, whilst a few others went into storage for some years. One such, when it was registered for the road in 1964, (fitted with the *second* of two saloon bodies by Maurice Gomm) became the last all-new Jowett to be completed. However, although this car is still with us, since the early 1970s it has been clothed in standard bodywork following crash damage. Thanks to this unfortunate turn of fate, the first of the Maurice Gomm saloons was elevated to the position of the youngest all-new Jowett in existence: it was completed in 1960, curiously with its coachwork fitted to only the twenty-fourth production chassis.

The youngest surviving all-new Jowett. Tim Wheater (left), current owner, talking to the car's designer Geoff Clarke. (Wheater)

7 Le Mans – and Monte Carlo Again

Mud-stained Jupiter of Tommy Wise and Horace Grimley on arrival at Monaco, 1951 International Monte Carlo Rally. Notice the single hand-operated screen wiper above the screen to supplement the unreliable Lucas device; also electric demisters to supplement the Smiths heater. The starting-handle eye looks as if it has seen much use. (LAT Photographic)

The Le Mans 24-Hour road race was conceived in the early 1920s by Georges Durand, secretary of the Automobile Club de l'Ouest (ACO), Emile Coquille and the young Charles Faroux, editor of *La Vie Automobile*, who were all concerned about the reliability and efficiency of the production cars of the day. Hence the decision to run a day–night race in order not only to test round-the-clock endurance, but also to stimulate the development of electrics and headlights, then still prone to breakdowns. The ACO agreed to organize such a race, on the outskirts of Le Mans in the Département of Sarthe, for cars that were as close as possible to production models. In 1923 the first Grand Prix d'Endurance was run on

May 26 and 27, its start baptized by a tempestuous rainstorm accompanied by hail; subsequently, with two exceptions, it has always been held in June. The race has been run every year since, apart from 1936 (either because the Spanish civil war was raging, or because of a general strike – reports differ), and between 1940 and 1948 when World War II intervened. Traditionally the start is at 16:00 on the Saturday after a week of testing, scrutineering, final adjustments and practice.

The rules had become extremely detailed by 1950, running to twenty pages and seventy-five articles in small type. The race was open to series production touring and sports cars as before, but since the previous year prototypes were allowed

– it was taken on trust that these would lead to series production, even though there was no way to enforce this. Over time, this rule would alter the character of the event entirely. The race was still intended to simulate touring, with all the special Le Mans rules: for example, in the event of some failure out on the circuit, only the driver was allowed to work on the car (with no advice permitted); at the pits two nominated mechanics were permitted, but they could only use spares carried in the car; refuelling was only allowed in the pits; and most importantly, on entering the pits the engine had to be stopped, and before rejoining the fray it had to fire up on the button – push starts or using the starting handle were definitely not allowed. The pit counter separates the pit from the track, and only a few things were allowed on it, such as a jack, oil draining pan, coolant and oil funnels, and a wet cloth for cleaning the windscreen.

Distance checks were made every 4 hours in order to disqualify cars that were not maintaining their prescribed pace, this being decided on engine capacity. As conservative as the qualifying distances seemed, there was good reason for it: Le Mans was then, and still is, a gruelling endurance test, and any of a number of factors, such as electrical failure, brake fade, engine fatigue or just plain poor driving, could contribute to disquali-

fication. Accordingly, the finishing rate for Le Mans is not high – and in 1931 it was only a meagre six!

Grandfield spoke good French and was able to study the race regulations in their original language, going through them with a fine toothcomb. The Le Mans Jupiter would therefore be as light and as fast as the rules allowed, whilst carrying nothing superfluous. Bodywork was formed from 18g aluminium compared with 16g for the standard road car, the doors were just bare aluminium shells, there was no interior trim, the basic instrument panel was dominated by the rev counter, there was one lightweight load-bearing racing seat for the driver and one mock seat (for lightness), beneath a thin aluminium half-tonneau cover (for its aerodynamic properties). The single aero screen was swept by a tiny electric wiper blade; even the rear-view mirror was behind a small fairing. The headlights were Lucas 770 with flat glass lenses: these had streamlining bowls over them for daytime running, and would have needed yellow bulbs to comply with French road-going regulations. A conventional oil cooler of the largest feasible size was in the conventional place, right at the front in the airflow. There were no strakes on the front or rear wings, and of course, no trafficators. The normal cast-iron brake drums were replaced by

Final pit checks before the off, 1950 Le Mans. In the background Mike Wilson (with towel) is standing in front of the fire extinguisher with Tommy Wise, while Grandfield (white shirt) and Grimley (braces) talk to a race official. Note the mirror fairing and water radiator cap on the Jupiter; in the background the elephant's trunk fuel pipe. (Collection Joves)

proprietary finned aluminium ('Alfin') drums, and these stood up well to the rigours of circuit racing. Two petrol tanks filled the tail to give at least 6 hours running between pitstops, with the aim of saving vital time.

The bonnet was pierced by an external water-filler cap, two four-louvre panels, and slots for the leather securing straps that were required by the regulations. Although it was held down at the front by quick-release clamps, unnecessary raising of the bonnet could cost valuable time, so for oil-level checking and refilling, the entire (sealable) centre grille could be removed from the front. In this way all three fluids could be refilled without unstrapping the bonnet, and the seals are a reminder that replenishment was only allowed at the pits, and the plombeur or pit policeman in each pit was there to refix the lead seals and check that they had not been tampered with out on the circuit.

On this occasion the car was to be driven by Tom Wisdom and Tommy Wise, and some person unknown sign-wrote 'Sagacious II' on the bonnet on both sides. Tom Wisdom was a Le Mans veteran, having had his first encounter with the circuit in 1933 when, as a young whipper-snapper, he was teamed with Mortimer Morris Goodall in an

Aston Martin. He then had four years spanning 1934–39 driving a Singer, finishing eighteenth overall in 1934. For the 1949 season not only did he crew the victorious Spa Javelin (as is recounted elsewhere), but he co-drove H. S. F. Hay's 1939 4¼-litre Bentley to sixth overall on the Sarthe circuit at an average speed of 73.56mph (118.36km/h); two Simcas broke their crank in that race. So he brought considerable endurance-racing skills with him to the Jowett team, and in addition he was a widely read motoring journalist which, it was hoped, would ensure useful publicity if all went well for the Yorkshire entry. Tommy Wise, as already noted, had rally and trials experience behind him, beginning in 1933 with an Allard trials special.

Le Mans 1950

At the circuit the Jowett team rubbed shoulders with some very well known drivers, including Sidney Allard himself with one of his own cars, Leslie Johnson and Bert Hadley (Jaguar), George Abecassis and Lance Macklin (Aston Martin), the Rosier father and son team with their Lago Talbot – a very thinly disguised racing car presumably

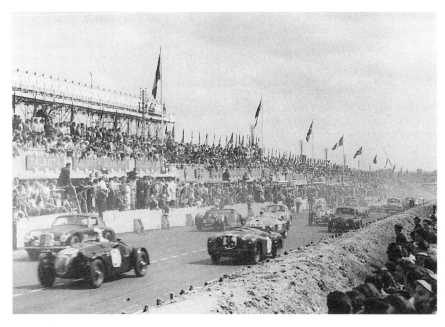

Pit scene seconds after the start. (Washington Photo)

Flying helmet and goggles for Tom Wisdom in Sagacious II. (Collection Joves)

running under the prototype rule: it had separate wings attached to the suspension, separate lighting, and just about seating for two – and Fangio and Gonzales who were to drive a very rapid, super-charged Simca Gordini. Other Simca Gordinis were driven by Maurice Trintignant, Jean Behra and Aldo Gordini. Jacques Savoye, who later sold Jupiters, was racing a 611cc Monopole.

The 1,101 to 1,500cc class comprised the Jupiter, two 1,491cc Simca Gordinis, a 1,483cc Fiat and the 1,244cc rebodied lightweight MG TC of George Phillips and Eric Winterbottom. The MG's special very skimpy coachwork did not even have a passenger door, for at that time open cars at Le Mans only needed one. The Simca Gordinis were very light, practicable road vehicles, and were very fast – Trintignant reached sixth in the early stages in the other supercharged version – but unreliable.

For the famous 'Le Mans Start', much imitated in those days wherever sports cars raced, the drivers stood opposite their cars on the pit straight on circles painted on the tarmac; the cars were parked diagonally with engines stopped and doors closed. When Charles Faroux let the tricolour fall at 4pm, they sprinted across, jumped in, pressed the starter button and swept away – straight into an enormous high-speed traffic jam.

The Jowett tactic was to drive for 6-hour spells, a novel plan because in those days the drivers normally raced in 3- or at most 4-hour stints. The thin aluminium half-tonneau cover must have proved unsuitable, as it was not used. It is apparent through photographic evidence that the headlamp fairings were employed on Saturday and Sunday, so there must have been quick pitstops to remove them at dusk and refit them at dawn.

In the 1,500cc class the first retirement was the

André Simon/Aldo Gordini Simca Gordini at 6 hours with gearbox trouble, to be followed a couple of hours later by their team-mates Roger Loyer/Jean Behra with a distributor fault. The Jupiter now assumed the class lead with two-thirds of the race still ahead, and as cars fell out, the Jupiter gradually moved up in the general category, to mounting excitement in the Jowett camp. As so often at Le Mans, there was thick fog during the night, something that suited the rally drivers amongst the competitors. When after eleven hours racing the Fiat retired, also with gearbox trouble, the class became an all-British affair, with the Jupiter heading the MG. And so it remained for the rest of an uneventful race – at least for *Sagacious II* – except perhaps for Sunday's torrential rainstorm that made the track slippery in the afternoon.

Louis Rosier, driving 23 out of the 24 hours, won the race for France, the last time a French car and driver would take the top honour until Henri Pescarolo and Graham Hill in a Matra Simca in 1972. The MG with its works-prepared engine had averaged 73mph (117km/h) – about the top speed of a normal TC – while the Jupiter in its debut race, in front of a crowd estimated to be half a million, broke Aston Martin's record set in 1937 with an average of 75.8mph (121.9km/h), nine laps in front of the MG. Wisdom obliged with a long article and action photo of the Javelin Jupiter in the London Daily Herald on the day following the win: the Jupiter, he reported, had put in an 80mph (129km/h) lap, and had clocked 100mph (160km/h) down the Mulsanne straight.

Monte Carlo 1951

The dream start to the Jupiter's competition career at Le Mans seemed to vindicate the Eberhorst frame and those who saw the car as basically a racing machine. The Jupiter was put into limited production while the chance to test the opposing point of view came with the Monte Carlo Rally, billed as the biggest rally ever staged.

Eleven Jowetts had contested the Monte Carlo Rally in 1950, with Tommy Wise and Mike Wilson returning with a Javelin. The *Bradford Telegraph & Argus* had telephoned Tommy's family to find out about progress, but the answer to their question 'Is there any news?' was: 'It's a girl!' – for

Late in 1950, Grandfield, Grimley and GKW 111 reconnoitre the Monte Carlo Rally route. (LAT Photographic)

Jupiter team for the 1951 Monte. Left to right: Bob Ellison and Bill Robinson, Gordon Wilkins and Raymond Baxter, and Horace Grimley and Tommy Wise. (JCL Publicity)

Tommy Wise's daughter Nikki was born during the event. Perhaps not, but then perhaps in part encouraged by this good news, at the finish his had been the highest placed Javelin. Even then he could only manage class fifteenth, and so for 1951, the factory involvement concentrated on the Jupiter.

So again the Jupiter was following in the tyre marks of the Javelin, and a team of three was prepared by the factory again after a careful study of the detailed rules and regulations which, amongst many other things, stipulated that the cars should be exactly to the catalogue specification. The rally's stated aim was to sort out the best cars for winter touring and one of the rules, which tended to favour French makes, was that servicing could only be carried out at a franchised dealer. If a works team was entered, this was partially overcome by signing up garages for the duration at critical points on the route: for example Jowett engaged a garage in Clermont Ferrand for any preparation that might have been needed for the final run down to Monaco.

It was also necessary that all work be carried out during driving time, and the best drivers drove hard and fast to give themselves time in hand either for servicing or for off-road sleep. In order to win the rally or achieve a high placing it was necessary to arrive at Monte Carlo without penalty, because the top places were awarded to the unpenalized, with the final order determined by their performance in the two special tests at Monaco. There was a total of over fifty prizes on offer, such as the coveted Charles Faroux Cup awarded to the leading nominated team of three cars of the same make, and the various trophies awarded by motoring-related product manufacturers, publications or clubs. Horace Grimley and Charles Grandfield reconnoitred the route in early January, taking the ex-Le Mans car GKW 111, now rebuilt as a standard touring Jupiter.

For the 1,500cc category there was strong opposition from the Simcas, several crewed by racing drivers such as Behra and Scaron (and with Trintignant their team manager). The Jowett entry totalled thirteen, with seven starting from Glasgow, of which four were Jupiters. Three formed the works team of Tommy Wise/Horace Grimley, Bill Robinson/Bob Ellison and Raymond Baxter/Gordon Wilkins, in company with the privately entered Jupiter of K. B. Miller. The

Glasgow Javelins were crewed by Les Odell/John Marshall, Nelson-Harris and Lawry/Smeeton – the latter had four yellow headlamps, a spotlamp, and a roof-rack with two snow-chained spare wheels. The French Jupiter of Thévenin/Campuon started from Lisbon, and the Jupiters of Spaniards Fabricas Bas/Iglesias and Dutchmen Scheffer/Willing, in company with two Javelins, started from Monte Carlo. A Norwegian Javelin started from Oslo. This total of seven Jupiters entered is especially remarkable since by the end of 1950 only thirteen had been constructed and two of these were in North America.

Entrants had to average above 31mph (50km/h) and below 37mph (60km/h) between the dozen or so controls on each of the six routes, which implied roughly 16-hour driving spells over 4 days, often actually at night – for example the Glasgow starters left the Amsterdam control at one-minute intervals from 2:34am, and Le Puy on the final run in to Monte Carlo from 1:23am. Typically just one hour of sleep each night could be snatched during the 4-day, 3-night run. The seemingly modest 31mph had to cover all stops – food, petrol, border controls, losing the way, repairs and all the other delays that long-distance touring involves, so attempting to sleep in a car piloted by the co-driver was normal. Early arrivals were, of course, of great benefit to the restaurant trade. Raymond Baxter was a BBC correspondent, and he was met at each control by an outside broadcast van for his report, putting further pressure on Wilkins to get the Jupiter in with time in hand. When leaving a control, competitors generally received motorcycle escorts through the main towns and cities, often with speed limits waived by the local constabulary. The Paris control was just off the Place de l'Etoile in front of the offices of the motoring paper *l'Action Automobile*, with its bar crowded with chatting competitors and their acolytes.

K. B. Miller's Jupiter was prone to gasket blowing, and true to form, it blew another one after less than 100 miles (160km) and he retired at the Carlisle control. Willing and Scheffer's Jupiter retired after about 1,400 miles (2,250km) at the Brussels control after losing a fan (Jowetts seemed

to have more than their share of trouble with this component) and suffering oil loss, suggesting the chassis-mounted oil cooler might have been damaged by the fan.

Competitors were troubled by black ice in Holland, but that apart, the good weather in the early stages gave way to heavy falls of snow in central and southern France, especially near Castellane and the Col de Lèques, with cars slithering about desperately trying to maintain the average. The Jupiters proceeded in a succession of controlled slides, both uphill and down – Tommy Wise with his trialling experience was in his element here. The Castellane blizzard brought down a telegraph pole just before the Ellison/Robinson Jupiter came through, but they somehow managed to avoid a serious tangle with the wires. On one slippery stretch a non-competing Renault held up a queue of rally cars until two competitors got out and manhandled it into a ditch! The Jupiter crews decided to save precious time by not stopping to fit the snow-chained wheels – instead they juggled past other hopelessly stuck competitors who had taken the same decision. The lower slopes from Grasse were in blinding rain: nevertheless, hopes that the rally would be decided more or less on the road section by winter weather were not fully realized, and 108 out of the 337 starters reached the Principality unpenalized.

The rules decreed that the cars without road penalties should fill the top places in the finishing order, the actual order being decided by two tests at Monaco. Open cars had to have their hoods raised for both. The first was the acceleration/braking/reverse/forward (ABRF) test that all competitors (road penalties or not) took immediately upon arrival, typically in a state of exhaustion. The fifty best road-unpenalized competitors from the ABRF test then went through to the second test, which comprised six timed laps of the Monaco Grand Prix circuit from a standing start, and this defined the top fifty positions in the general category. Since there were 108 competitors without road penalty, the next fifty-eight competitors' positions were defined by their ABRF points alone, while the remaining

*Javelin during the acceleration/
braking/reverse/forward test on a
wet early morning at Monaco.
(LAT Photographic)*

places were calculated from a combination of road marks and the results of the ABRF test.

The ABRF test comprised accelerating for 200m from a standstill, stopping with the front wheels over a line, reversing to behind the line, and then accelerating for a further 50m. The overall time for this manoeuvre was measured to a tenth of a second. Helpfully the RAC had set up a replica of this test at Silverstone a few weeks earlier, so that serious British competitors had practised; even carburettor experts had been on hand to assist. The Jowett team had worked hard on this trial of a certain sort of driving skill. An important factor here was the slickness of first/reverse gear changing, and the Javelin/Jupiter steering column mechanism can be set up to be quite good in this respect.

The unpenalized finishers included the three works Jupiters, and the Odell/Marshall and Nelson-Harris Javelins. Early arrivals, which it so happened included these five Jowetts, found the tarmac waterlogged and slippery from the overnight rain. Robinson, Wilkins and Odell, using every rev the engine would give and using all the brakes they dared in the damp conditions, did well enough to qualify for the final eliminator;

unfortunately Tommy Wise's Jupiter broke a fuel pipe whilst reversing and could only splutter over the line, so losing the Jowett team the prospect of winning the Charles Faroux cup.

The cars were then locked away in the parc fermé for the following day's critical examination for compliance, faults and body damage, any of which could lose vital points. Now at last the crews could get some real sleep!

The final test was as near as you like to a production car race ever organized in a rally and it favoured the faster cars and the racing drivers. The last four laps of the six were timed, and a complicated formula took into account both how quickly they were executed, and the regularity – that is, the variation between the laps. The trick was to drive as quickly as possible from the off and to match each subsequent lap to lap two. Local man Louis Chiron ($4\frac{1}{2}$-litre Delahaye) was expected to win this event, but in fact it went to fellow racing driver Jean Trevoux in another Delahaye. In one of his laps the Hotchkiss driver Marcel Becquart (last year's outright winner in that make) overcooked the chicane on the seafront, bounced off a pylon, the spare wheel flew off into the sea and his car very nearly followed.

Prize-giving at Monaco. Robinson with the Riviera Cup, snapped by Ellison. The tyres are Wyresoles. (Collection Joves)

John Marshall expertly diced Odell's Javelin round the course, while Robinson put the Jupiter right into the frame as he hurled his car through with some brilliantly fast laps, quicker even than Wilkins in the other qualifying Jupiter.

Indeed, Robinson's best lap of 2min 31sec made him the fastest British competitor, a full three seconds quicker than the best Simca; Maurice Trintignant, who smelled a rat, was furious and demanded that the Jupiters be inspected by the authorities. This included an engine capacity measurement, but the Jupiters were found to be completely standard. They had clearly been well driven, but equally clearly the Jupiter's handling on the tight Monaco circuit was very advanced for its day.

In all, ten of the thirteen Jowetts were classified as finishers. The confirmed results put the Ellison/Robinson Jupiter as class winner at equal sixth (with Ken Wharton's Ford Pilot) in the general classification, with Wilkins and Baxter second at tenth, and Les Odell's Javelin fourth at twenty-sixth. The best that Trintignant's much-fancied Simcas could manage was class third at sixteenth in the general classification.

For winning the 1,500cc class, the Ellison/Robinson Jupiter collected the Riviera Cup, the Coupe Cibié for the class, the Calculateur Road-ex Award for the class, the Stuart Trophy and, with Ken Wharton, the Tyresoles Challenge Cup (for the best performance by a member of the Monte Carlo Rally British Competitors' Club, irrespective of tyres). The top three Jowetts together won the *l'Action Automobile* Challenge for the highest placed three cars of the same make in the 1,500cc class.

Ellison and Robinson donated the cup to Jowett, and were promised a replica each. Expenses for the rally could be claimed back but had to be submitted to Norman Snell, the company secretary, who was noted for his stinginess. Horace Grimley warned Ellison '…put your expenses up a bit because Snell will knock them down again.' When the replica cups arrived they were two inches high!

Le Mans 1951

Jowett fielded a team of three Jupiters for the 1951 Le Mans, all specially built for the race. Two

Runners-up Wilkins (left) and Baxter collect their trophy at Monte Carlo in 1951. (LAT Photographic)

were lightweight standard cars (constructed very much along the lines of last year's success story) with a special cut-down racing version called the R1 to make up the trio. The R1 was based on a simplified and narrowed version of the Eberhorst frame with rather primitive, skimpy bodywork incorporating cycle wings at the front; it was registered HAK 364 and was piloted by Wisdom and

Road test: Grimley carries out an adjustment to Hadley's Jupiter, while Grandfield (white shirt) and Hadley (back to camera) look on. Becquart's Hotchkiss is on the extreme left, his Jupiter behind Hadley's. GKW 111, tender car, is on the extreme right. (Becquart)

Jowett and the International Lisbon Rally

A Javelin crewed by Tommy Wise and Mike Wilson took class second in the 1950 Lisbon, in spite of a persistent misfire from Paris. The most important Lisbon International Rally for Jowett was the one held the following year, from 1 to 7 May 1951. As usual cars left ten starting points in nine countries and covered about 2,000 miles (3,200km), as was usual with the international rallies of the day. There were two categories, touring and sports, with the usual capacity subdivisions and the proviso that open cars had to be true dropheads. There were only fifteen British competitors, of whom the best known were Ken Wharton (Ford V8 Pilot) who already had two outright wins under his belt, and Goff Imhoff (Allard), both starting from Frankfurt. Another British competitor had neglected to obtain a visa for Portugal and had to retire his Bristol at the border. There was just one Jupiter entered, that of the Portuguese driver Joaquim Filipe Nogueira, and he had no factory backing. Torrential rain fell between Bordeaux and San Sebastian (leading to Imhoff's retirement), there was fog in the Spanish mountains, and sunshine at the finish.

At the end of the road section, Nogueira was lying second overall to the Ford Pilot of Clemente Meneres, the next two cars being a Simca and a Porsche. After the road section there were two days of tests and trials, which enabled Nogueira, in a superb exhibition of fast, sure driving in the very last of the tests, to edge ahead of Meneres to take the rally outright, and with it the award for the highest placed Portuguese driver. The 1,086cc Porsche was relegated to fifth, while Ken Wharton came in sixth.

For 1952, Nancy Mitchell, Bea Norman and Joyce Leavens (in the Leavens Javelin) had a good rally in spite of having to divert from their route: this was due to severe rain and floods from San Sebastian on the French/Spanish border. Joyce later claimed that during one night they just kept heading westwards, using the stars for navigation! Nancy Mitchell drove in the final tests at Estoril, while Joyce, sliding about on the bench seat, navigated and handled the stopwatches. At the finish the three were the highest placed ladies team, and were awarded the Coupe des Dames at eleventh in class. The two locally crewed Jupiters could manage only class seventh and ninth. Nogueira again won, but this time in a Porsche.

For 1953 the Lisbon International was moved to October. Nogueira (Porsche) again won, and the event is really only notable in our story because it was the last time a Jupiter contested an international rally: Maurice Tew finished overall twenty-fifth, about eighth in the 2-litre open car class, his Jupiter one place ahead of a Javelin.

Relaxing in Le Mans. Bert Hadley, far left. (Becquart)

Scrutineering the coachwork section in a basketball hall in Le Mans. The two standard Jupiters, bonnets lifted, can be made out on the left. (Becquart)

Wise. The two 'standard' Jupiters were registered HAK 365 for Marcel Becquart and Gordon Wilkins, and HAK 366 for Bert Hadley and Charles Goodacre.

Both Hadley and Goodacre had competed at Le Mans in 1937, whilst in 1950 Hadley and Leslie Johnson had shared the XK120 that retired from third place with a bare three hours to go. Hadley was still one of the fastest British drivers of his day, but at the war's end he had decided against a professional motor-racing career in favour of a normally paid one. He felt motivated to offer his services and enormous expertise (gained as an Austin apprentice and in the pre-war Austin racing workshops) and skill to the new boy on the block, Jowett, so he turned down the repeat offer from Jaguar, and here he was in the Jupiter team. Soon after arriving at the Sarthe circuit for practice he crossed swords with Grandfield: the R1 had, at 65bhp, a more highly tuned engine, a higher back axle ratio, and lighter coachwork with a lower frontal area than the standard Jupiters, and he had assumed that as the fastest driver he would be given the fastest car – but not so: Wisdom the journalist took precedence.

Gordon Wilkins, paired with Becquart, was also a journalist, although at sixth reserve was not yet guaranteed a race.

Marcel Becquart was born in the Wallonian part of Belgium, but was now French and living in Annecy, running his own business making fashionable up-market watch straps. His ties with Hotchkiss, for whom he had rallied in the Montes of 1949, 1950 and 1951, were loosening, as Hotchkiss was in difficulties as a car-maker and indeed would be absorbed by Delage in 1952. Harry Ainsworth, who had managed Hotchkiss pre-war and had re-established that make in the car market in 1947, had become close friends with Becquart and together they looked at the Javelin at a Geneva motor show – Geneva being on Becquart's doorstep. Becquart, impressed by the Javelin he test-drove, was persuaded that the Jupiter with its Eberhorst frame would be even better. He decided to throw in his lot with Jowett, and to further his ambition to race at Le Mans in 1951 he ordered a Jupiter chassis to be sent for bodying to Stabilimenti Farina in Turin. It so happened that full hydraulic braking was still under development at that time, and there were delays in shipping the chassis. But Jowett were not going to let such a big fish go, so Becquart was offered a works drive at Le Mans, and the Farina went back to Turin to be modified to comply with Monte Carlo rally regulations.

All the reserves were called up, and all three Jowetts took to the circuit. Wisdom started badly, getting his foot tangled in the R1's steering column, so Hadley got away first and was initially the faster of the two; but after ten laps, having proved a point, he slowed to let Wisdom past. Gonzales (Talbot) almost from the start headed the youthful Stirling Moss (Jaguar XK120C) to enthusiastic applause from the huge crowd; then, sensationally, Moss passed Gonzales to set a new lap record and lead the race until after midnight. In the 1,500cc class the four 85bhp Simca-Gordinis set up a furious pace and began to open up a big lead on the MG. This specially built car from Abingdon was mechanically a TDII clothed in aluminium, streamlined, prototype MGA bodywork sitting rather awkwardly on its TD chassis. The R1 fell in behind the MG, and the other two Jupiters followed. Wilkins later commented that although his car was down on acceleration, '… there were not many cars that could get away from the Jupiter in the winding stretches. Several times I went drifting fast into the swerves before Arnage, with a much faster car behind, and by the time it emerged the Jupiter had gained several lengths.'

Unfortunately after a mere nineteen laps Hadley was the second retirement from the race, the first from the class, with a broken valve collar, something he maintained he could have fixed had he been carrying the right spares – another quarrel with Grandfield. When Hadley failed to reappear, his teammate Goodacre set out to find him and asked him what was wrong; so according to the regulations Hadley was disqualified for being given verbal advice. It was something of an anomaly that the three Cunninghams were in

The 1951 R1 somewhere in Le Mans wearing its roundel that signifies it is an entrant in the Biennial Cup. All eyes turned to the cameraman. Grandfield (standing) and Wise (seated). (Washington Photo)

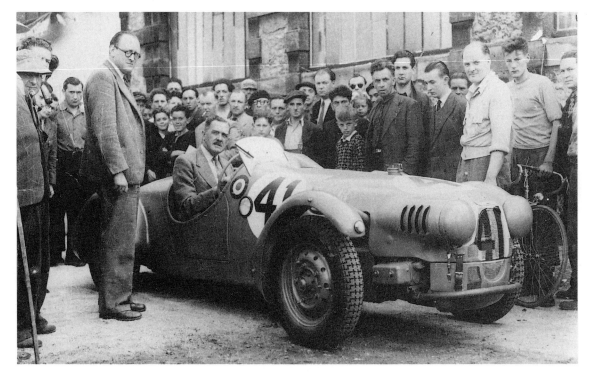

(Above and below) The Javelin's clean, balanced lines needed little change through its seven-year production life.

(Right) The well laid-out instrument panel of the de Luxe model, showing the 'clear vision' steering wheel.

The headlamps fitted to this 1952 Javelin were an optional extra.

Front passenger door, showing the elbow rest.

Two-tier tool tray close to hand.

Concealed within the Javelin's elegant rear is a more than adequate boot.

The flowing lines of the Jupiter – this is a 1952 example.

(Above left) The tail conceals interior space for two suitcases.

(Above)Flashing indicators are of course a common addition to cars dating back to the early 1950s.

(Left) Another view of the 1952 Jupiter.

The owners have a range of suitcases for the rack, depending on the length of the holiday.

Bench seat theoretically takes three but is upholstered for two.

Spare wheel accessibility is good; the clipped-in wheel-brace is an owner's modification.

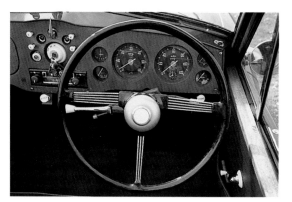

Driver's view of the very complete instrumentation – it includes an oil temperature gauge.

Door trim includes map pocket.

The unmistakeably Italian lines of the R4 Jupiter.

The front end of this low-cost sports car is fabricated from a composite resin-impregnated fabric material.

(Above) This saloon Jupiter, constructed by Adams & Robinson, was once owned by John Willment of Willment Bros. (Dave Burrows)

(Left) The R4 has a compact engine bay thanks to the format of the flat-four engine and radiator over the gearbox. The electric cooling fan was part of the original design package.

(Above and above right) The business-like R4 cockpit layout.

The Jupiter of Mike Smailes
heads the TD of Eric Benson
at a Silverstone event for
historic sports cars. (Chris
Harvey)

The Javelin of Geoff
McAuley and Frank Woolley
during the 1988 Pirelli
Classic Marathon at Pirelli's
Vizzola Ticino test track
near Milan. This quick run
promoted the car to class
second – temporarily!
(Peter Cahill)

Gerald Palmer, his self-designed house, and the two cars for which he is best remembered. On the left is the MG Magnette.
(Gary Stuart)

The sumptuous interior of the de Luxe Javelin, as depicted in one of the company's sales brochures.

continuous radio contact with their pit, a situation not covered by the letter of that particular law.

The quickest Simca put in its best lap of 94.23mph (151.62km/h), over 10mph (16km/h) faster than the MG and the R1 at 83.81 (134.85) and 83.37 (134.14) respectively. The R1, however, blew a gasket after five hours, and with the MG melting a piston just before nightfall, and the Simcas as usual experiencing engine troubles of their own, it was left to Becquart and Wilkins to hold their nerves. By daybreak there was just one Simca left, nine laps ahead of the Jowett. Soon its engine failed, and the Jowett pit signalled that the Jupiter should reduce speed. It toured to finish at a modest 71.15mph (144.48) average, the only finisher in class and twenty-second in the general category. The overall winner was the Walker/Whitehead Jaguar at 93.49mph (150.43km/h).

Monte Carlo 1952

This was an important event for Jowett, not only with the 1949 and 1951 wins to live up to, but also because the Jupiter was now available in quantity at home, just as the Commonwealth markets of Australia, New Zealand and Canada were shutting up shop with protectionist import policies. Rally regulations no longer allowed open cars, but specially constructed closed examples on chassis of series production open cars were permitted just for this year and next. The six routes were much the same although the final part was longer, with a quite difficult section through St Flour, the upshot being that from Le Puy to Valence competitors would have to drive fast. There was no ABRF test this year, and instead of the regularity/speed test on the Monaco GP circuit, the final (and in fact only) test was a regularity run held around a twisty 47-mile (75km) circuit over the Col de Braus in the mountains above Monaco; it was split into four very different sections, and you had to complete each one in as close as possible to equal times.

This was a typical test in rallies of the day, and it favoured those such as Gatsonides who could take time off to practise it. Jowett relied heavily

Marcel Becquart at the wheel of his Farina Jupiter. As usual he chose the Lisbon start. (Collection Joves)

on Becquart and his Farina Jupiter, whilst the service department provided some support to private entrants. The Farina was driven to England for a thorough overhaul, a replacement engine, and some other parts to ensure the car was as near perfect as Grandfield and his men could make it. The nominated team of three Jupiters for the Charles Faroux Cup comprised the Farina, the French-built saloon Jupiter of Jean Latune (president of the Auto Club de la Drôme) and the Swiss-built saloon for Thévenin. The latter, unfortunately, unhappy with the preparation of the car by the French Jowett agent Plissons, scratched at the last minute. Another Jupiter specially built for the rally and with a little factory support was the privately entered Farr-bodied Jupiter of Robert Ellison, this year co-driven by his friend Walter Mason.

The Glasgow start witnessed six Javelins, including that of Mrs Vaughan with Mrs Ashfield as co-driver. At the age of sixty-nine, this was Mrs Vaughan's seventh Monte. One of the strongest contenders was the Javelin of Frank and Lola Grounds, running with Jupiter wheels and headlights that were presumably acceptable to the rally organizers as they were deemed to be available as standard options. Ellison in his Farr Jupiter also started from Glasgow. The fancied Javelin of TT motorcycle champion Bob Foster and

The RAC-TT

The RAC International Tourist Trophy Race for sports cars, held in September 1951, was the most convincing sports car race for Jupiters in Britain. Car racing on public roads was not allowed on the British mainland, but up to the mid-1950s it did still take place on the Isle of Man, Jersey and in Northern Ireland.

The RAC-TT course was on the outskirts of Belfast in Northern Ireland, and it was a dangerous one. The circuit was formed from country lanes bordered by stone walls, hard earth banks and ditches, there were tricky bends and fast curves, real hills and a fast straight along which the cars were timed. The cars were divided into four capacity classes, and the race was run on a handicap basis of credit laps. The race length was 319 miles (513km) and was expected to take four hours; the winner on handicap would be awarded the Tourist Trophy. Cars had to be standard as catalogued, with at least ten produced for sale. There are lies, damned lies and the things motor sportsmen tell you, for this rule did not prevent the participation of three MG-engined specials in the Jupiter's class as well as the Aston Martin DB3 prototype (constructed on a chassis designed by Eberan-Eberhorst) in another group.

The Jupiter entries comprised the works team of Bert Hadley, Tom Wisdom and Tommy Wise, accompanied by the youthful Bill Skelly in his own car. The class competition came from the three-man works MG TDII team plus three private MGs and a Cooper-MG, all with engines displacing 1,250cc, and a pair of Lester-MGs with engines bored to 1,467cc. There could not have been any Porsches, for although a few 1,300cc examples did exist at that time, they were for road and rally use, and not for racing.

All three works Jupiters had run at Le Mans: Wise was in GKW 111, the hero of 1950, Hadley drove his 1951 car and Wisdom the Becquart/Wilkins 1951 class winner. The MGs and the Cooper-MG, having a lower capacity, had a shorter distance to cover than the Jupiters and the Lesters. During practice Hadley was noticeably the quickest of the Jupiter men, and managed to set the same time as the fastest Lester-MG.

When the race got going Stirling Moss in an XK120C immediately set the pace and went on to take the trophy.

Tourist trophy for the 1,500cc class winner.
(Collection Joves)

Lance Macklin in the DB3 had to retire when holding second well ahead of the DB2s, the Allards and the rest of the Jaguars. In the 1,500cc class the two Lester-MGs, too highly tuned to last, went out with differing engine failures, and two MGs were forced out with various bothers. This left the Cooper-MG, the Jupiters with Hadley the star performer and four TDs. After two hours Hadley began to pass the MGs, and at the finish the class positions were Hadley (68.71mph (110.55km/h)), Wise (68.59mph (110.36km/h)), Reece in the Cooper-MG (67.63mph (108.81km/h)) with the highest placed of a quartet of surviving MGs fourth (66.24mph (106.58km/h)). After many pitstops for oil and water, Wisdom's Jupiter crossed the finishing line with what may well have been a failing head gasket, but to be classified 'still running at the finish'. His very public verbal abuse of Charles Grandfield ensured that this was his last race for Jowett.

The cars were timed on the main straight. Wise was quickest in the class at 92.9mph (150.0km/h), with Hadley next at 91.2mph (146.7km/h) and Wisdom managing 90.6 (145.8). The fastest MG was clocked at 83.8mph (134.8km/h).

Just to emphasize what a dangerous circuit this was, there was a driver fatality amongst the twelve who did not finish. That aside, this event and its high profile success were just what Jowett needed, coming as it did one bare month before the Jupiter's UK launch proper.

Becquart getting away at La Turbie during the regularity run in the mountains. (The Autocar)

George Holdsworth started from Munich, the Javelins of Johansson from Oslo, and the skilled ice-racer Norlander from Stockholm, whilst Becquart, as always, and Latune in their FHC Jupiters started from Lisbon.

As for the previous year, the weather was initially uneventful. The main drama for the Farina was a collision with a very large dog on the outskirts of Reims that did some damage to the car, crucially putting a headlamp out of action. No doubt the animal suffered, too. Paris was telephoned, and Becquart drove flat out to where a panel-beater was waiting. After basic work, Becquart took off and screamed into the Paris control with 10 seconds to spare. He then drove it to a garage for final fettling.

From Bourges to Valence the competitors were engulfed by a very severe snowstorm, heavier than most had ever encountered – it snowed heavily all over southern France and right along the Mediterranean coast, almost into Monaco itself. Many stopped to fit snow-chains, a time-consuming affair, especially by the road-side: you laid out the chains in front of the wheels, drove over them, let the air out of the tyres, fitted the chains and finally inflated the tyres again. Others just let some air out of the tyres and bravely pressed on regardless. One difficulty was dodging the car ahead when it spun out of control – on the downhill sections corner after corner had three or four cars tangled together. Mrs Vaughan saw her bid for the Ladies' Cup disappear when she managed to hole her Javelin's petrol tank, starting a fire. Some sections looked like the dead car park of a long distance race, so many slid off, crashed or were otherwise halted; the Farr Jupiter was one such. The Puy control had warned most competitors (but not Norlander) that the direct route to Valence was totally blocked by snow, and attempting this route and then having to double back lost the leading Javelin 8 minutes (80 points) at the next control. Only fifteen reached Monaco unpenalized to battle it out for the top honour but amongst them was Marcel Becquart's Jupiter.

For the regularity run, reminiscent of the one used in 1949, the roads were not closed to public traffic and dark-bodied cars had white distemper paint added to their fronts to increase their visibility. Again such heavy snow had fallen that one of the controls could not even be manned. This time the tables were turned and the Simca Sport of Dr and Mme Angelvin accrued less penalty points than Becquart to finish first in class at overall third, leaving Becquart in the leading Jowett class second at overall fifth. The unlucky Norlander was classified class ninth at overall 16th – the first of the road-penalized cars. The overall positions of the other finishing Jowett drivers were Foster 37th, Latune 58th, Grounds 61st, Odell 111th and Braid 147th.

The outright winner was Sydney Allard in an Allard Type P saloon, its only serious concession to rallying being the Dunlop Trakgrip tyres that were fitted all round. This was a unique triumph: a driver winning in a production car of his own make. Stirling Moss and two colleagues were second in a Sunbeam Talbot.

Le Mans 1952

It was by no means certain that Jowett would contest Le Mans in 1952. There was the likelihood that OSCA and Gordini would have improved their reliability, and of course Porsche was arriving. In 1951, the very first Porsche to race at the French circuit, a 1,086cc type 356 (running in another class), had finished 92km ahead of the Jupiter, and had indeed turned in its best lap of an astonishing 5min 44.7sec, compared with the R1's quickest of 6min 2sec. This year Porsche was to contest the 1,500cc class, and at this capacity it was obvious that it would present a very serious challenge.

Nevertheless, three R1s were prepared at the last minute. A new rule demanded all-enveloping bodywork, and so fronts were changed – but only just! The possibility of head gasket failure was eliminated by the fitting of Wills Rings liner/head seals, endless thin steel tubes filled during manufacture with a chemical giving off nitrogen when heated: the rings then expand, creating a perfect seal. Grandfield's men had succeeded in coaxing a little more power from the Jowett engine (significantly by raising the compression ratio to 9.25:1), but at 70bhp it was insufficient by a considerable margin to be regarded as competitive. Through poor reliability Gordini had lost the Simca contract and was entering two very fast cars under his own name, one in the

The three R1s at the Hôtel Saumon (the team's HQ) prior to the race. Left to right: Grandfield, Grimley, unknown, Harry Spears, Mike Wilson (timekeeper), unknown, Tommy Wise, Digger Metcalf, Peter Balderstone, Tom Bradley. Apart from Mike Wilson, all identified people were experimental department staff. (Collection Joves)

1,500cc class, while the other, at 2.3 litres actually, led the race for over 4 hours before retiring. In its post-war return to racing the Mercedes factory, sparing neither money nor men, had entered three cars and sent five, with no fewer than thirty-five mechanics. Tom Wisdom had seriously quarrelled with Grandfield over the preparation of his Jupiter at the Dundrod TT the previous summer, and was co-driving (with Leslie Johnson) a Nash Healey.

In the 1,500cc class, the Gordini lasted only twenty-six laps, to retire with engine or transmission failure, and the first Jowett retirement (Gatsonides), who had raced a lively race up to that point, followed at sixty-eight laps when the crankshaft broke on the Mulsanne straight. He had, though, set the fastest time by a Jowett, at 5min 51.4sec, 85.9mph (138.2km/h). The class honours were now being hotly disputed between the Porsche and the Ferrari-like 1,350cc OSCA saloon, with the R1 of Hadley and Wise some distance behind. The other R1, of Becquart and Wilkins, was in trouble with misfiring, and a drama lay ahead: after several pitstops the problem was traced to water and sand in the petrol, the contamination perhaps due to the thunderstorms that had struck Le Mans during the Saturday morning. This was not a new experience for Wilkins, as in the 1939 race his Singer had also been delayed with water in the petrol.

All petrol was provided by the ACO for each team. Behind the balconies positioned above the pits proper, there were tanks that supplied the fuel by gravity feed through a sort of elephant's trunk affair to give every competitor the same fuel at the same rate of flow. The tanks would have held 1,000 to 2,000 litres, and were regularly replenished by tanker trucks. Of course, no smoking was the rule without exception.

Becquart wanted to establish that it was the ACO, not Jowett, that was the cause of the poor running. He was concerned about the rule whereby each car had to achieve a set distance during each four-hour spell: things began to get heated, and he tipped a float-chamber's worth of water and sand onto the pit counter to convince the plombeur that the delay was the fault of the

ACO. Somewhat bizarrely the plombeur replied that water and sand were not on the list of things permitted to be placed on the pit counter, and suggested that the Jupiter could be excluded on that ground. Becquart exploded, and used a word of coarse French that cast aspersions on the manhood of the plombeur. This was too much, and Becquart had to retract, Charles Faroux was sent for to hear the apology, and indeed afterwards Becquart was obliged to write numerous letters to almost everyone involved with the race and motor sport. Nevertheless, the fuel lines were blown through, the tanks were flushed and refilled, the carburettors cleaned out, and the R1 continued, having lost the best part of an hour with no chance of winning the class or the biennial cup – or so it seemed.

A thick mist drifted across the cold, dank circuit in the early hours as Saturday's heavy rain evaporated. Levegh's Talbot was maintaining an unassailable lead over the two following Mercedes. Dawn broke to find the 1,500cc Porsche in some sort of trouble, for after holding the OSCA at bay for many hours, it was forced to reduce speed, letting the little Italian car cruise past to open up a useful lead. Then after nearly 16 hours Hadley's Jupiter expired, also with crank breakage. When eventually the OSCA's clutch broke, letting the Porsche through, the remaining Jupiter had a deficit of over twenty laps, and although gradually gaining on the German car, it could do little more than keep going and hope its crankshaft would remain in one piece.

There are two stories about what happened to the Porsche when it pitstopped with a little over 4 hours of the race left. One version has it that it failed to restart after the mandatory switch-off because the starter had failed. The other is that, knowing it would not restart, they tried to refuel the car with the engine running and were disqualified. Charles Faroux, the clerk of the course, seems to have been involved, but the disqualification (officially 'pitstop with engine running') stood, once again leaving the Jupiter just needing to tour to finish. The seemingly impregnable Talbot driven by Levegh (incredibly, it seems in retrospect, Levegh was aiming to drive the whole 24

Cockpit of the Becquart/Wilkins R1 restored to perfection. (Richard Keil)

After an ultimately successful third Le Mans campaign. Left to right: Gordon Wilkins, Charles Grandfield, Arthur Jopling and Marcel Becquart collect around the class winner. Bert Hadley far right. (Arthur Jopling)

hours himself) ran a big end with just an hour to go, letting the gull-wing Mercedes through to an astonishing one-two victory – but a victory greeted by muted applause. Only seventeen cars finished from the fifty-seven starters, of which four were British, the others being the Wisdom/Johnson Nash Healey in third place, a DB2 in seventh and a Frazer Nash in tenth.

Arthur Jopling was present during the race. He had budgeted for the three R1s and the Le Mans campaign, but he could see that Jowett had been very fortunate to snatch victory from the misfortunes of others, and that the R1, whatever its good points, was underpowered and that it seemed beyond Grandfield's capability to extract much more. He therefore announced that henceforth there would be no more Le Mans races for the Bradford company.

Typical wheel angles on a well set-up Jupiter as Becquart corners at speed during the regularity run. (Collection Joves)

Monte Carlo 1953

The rally in this year was run over the same routes as the previous year and had the same final test on the Col de Braus. It was noted for its good weather and its plethora of unpenalized arrivals at Monaco, no fewer than 253 out of 404 starters. One change was that 100 instead of fifty took part in the regularity run on the Col de Braus mountain roads. The ABRF test was reinstated.

The Jowett entries included Becquart again, in his works-prepared Farina Jupiter, his mistress Mme Sigrand with Mme Largeot in the factory Javelin HAK 743 competing for the Ladies Cup, Frank Grounds now in his attractive saloon Jupiter, another five Javelins, and Jean Latune's Jupiter. Becquart's hopes for an outright win or an improved position over last year were cruelly dashed when, during the regularity run, his Jupiter's rear fan support bracket broke and the

Frank Grounds on his way to class fourth, the 1953 International Monte Carlo Rally. (Grounds)

fan holed the radiator. This support bracket was perhaps the only component not subject to Grandfield's meticulous preparation schedule – it is a relatively flimsy affair designed by ERA, and was probably fatally weakened during the high-revving ABRF test at Monaco; this was the first instance of failure of this component, and today it is usually strengthened. Final Jowett placings were Frank Grounds (Jupiter) class fourth at 36th overall, Latune (Jupiter) sixth at 46th, Bob Foster (Javelin) 90th, Bill Pitcher (Javelin) 96th and two

Javelins tied for 171st place, namely Sigrand/ Largeot fifth in the Ladies Cup and Mr and Mrs Leavens. Becquart, in not finishing the Col de Braus test, was placed fifteenth in class at 98th. After superb preparation in every department, the rally was deservedly won outright by Maurice Gatsonides and Peter Worledge in a Ford Zephyr.

Becquart competed at Le Mans for a few more years, finishing fourteenth in 1953 with Wilkins in an Austin Healey 100, eleventh in 1954 with

Peter Dixon drives the 1952 class-winner in the 2001 Le Mans Legends race on the Sarthe 24-hour circuit. (Richard Keil)

Gatsonides in a Frazer Nash LM, and achieving his highest placing of tenth in 1955 in a Frazer Nash Sebring. He also continued with the Monte for several more years, co-driving with Maurice Gatsonides, but he never improved upon his 1950 Hotchkiss and 1952 Jowett results. His next best were sixth in 1958 in a TR3A, and seventh in 1955 in a DB2/4. Javelins continued to contest the Monte for a few more years, but the heady days for Jowett in these most classic of races and rallies were well and truly over.

8 Engineering Developments

Throughout the life of both the Javelin and the Jupiter, constant development took place to refine and improve the cars. We see elsewhere in this book the significant results attained in motor sport, and even from the first forays into competitive events, lessons were being learnt. Take, for example, the disintegrating cooling fan failures, which prevented what would likely have been a fine result for Javelins in the 1949 Alpine Rally. A revised fan design was introduced for the production cars within a few weeks of the event. Indeed, it was the Le Mans races that confirmed crankshaft weaknesses and led ultimately to the oval web design (paradoxically introduced after vehicle production ceased).

It is not the purpose of this chapter to list every minor modification in the cars' production lives. However, those changes that had an effect on performance, aesthetics or marketing of the cars are examined here in chronological order as applied to the Javelin. Where possible, for reference purposes the Javelin chassis number from which the modification was introduced is shown. This will assist current or potential owners in identifying what particular specification is relevant to a particular car. In most instances, any Javelin engine modifications that were applied during the production years of the Jupiter, were also relevant to the Jupiter.

The chassis numbering code of all post-war Jowetts followed a three-part scheme. The chassis number begins with an alphanumeric code, sequential letters signifying the decade with a number representing the actual year, as in 'D7' for 1947. So the calendar year of manufacture of a post-war Jowett car can be ascertained from the chassis number code.

The second part, the model type, is formed from two or three letters. For passenger cars, that is Javelins, the letters were PA, PB, PC, PD and PE, with the second letter signifying major model revisions. Sports cars, that is Jupiters, used SA and SC, where SA is for the Mk1 and SC for the Mk1a – there was no SB. A third letter, if present, would be L signifying 'left-hand drive'.

The third part of the chassis number is the chassis serial number. After this number the suffix D on a Javelin number would indicate 'de Luxe', while all Jupiters have a suffix R for no known reason. For both Javelins and Jupiters some chassis serial codes were not taken out, and the highest chassis number does not indicate the total number built. For example, the last Jupiter built has the serial number E4 SC 1033R, but the factory only constructed about 900.

Engineering Changes

Engineering change introduction points given below are from published Jowett documentation, and may not be exact in all cases.

Carburettors (from D9 PA 1753): The type was changed from Zenith 30VM4 to 30VM5. It is quite unusual now to find the earlier type.

Battery (from D9 PA 3696): Twin 6-volt batteries (one at each side of the car beneath the rear seat cushion) were replaced by a single 12-volt type in the nearside box.

Connecting rod bearings (from D9 PA 3794): Big-end bearing shells of copper-lead type were introduced, giving improved life.

Starter solenoid (from D9 PA 4243): Previously located at the rear of the starter motor, but now installed centrally beneath the floor, with a manual button accessible by the driver from within the car.

Main engine bearings (from D9 PA 4322): Now copper-lead type shells to the front and centre bearings. White metal shells remained on the rear bearing for the rest of the cars' production life.

Air filter (from D9 PA 5374): The oil-bath type was introduced, with a silencer/baffle box arrangement.

Model change (from D9 PA to D9 PB): The 1950 model, appearing from October 1949, saw the announcement of the first major cosmetic change to the Javelin. Two versions were offered (for the 1950 model year), the Javelin Saloon de Luxe and the Javelin Saloon. The de Luxe now offered an attractive wooden, walnut-veneered dashboard with full instrumentation (speedometer, clock, oil pressure, ammeter, fuel and water temperature gauges). High quality hide was used for the seat facings, and small touches, such as a passenger visor-mounted 'make-up' mirror, were included. A Smiths recirculation heater/demister was a standard fitment on this model.

Steering-arm ball joints (track-rod ends) (from D9 PB 6572): Height-adjustable type was introduced. Previously there was a choice of three steering balls of differing shank heights. Now any change in toe-in/toe-out of the front suspension with bump and rebound can be adjusted quickly and with precision – just one of the reasons why the handling of the Javelin and Jupiter was ahead of its time.

Crankshaft (from D9 PB 8902): The hardened type was fitted. This is significant because there is a suspicion that subsequent breakages were associated with the hardening of crankshafts. If this is so, then Palmer cannot be blamed for the failures, since the decision to harden the shafts was not his.

Front engine mountings (from E0 PB 10450): An improved version from Metalastik was introduced, identified by a central reinforcing plate bonded into the rubber block.

Connecting rods (from E0 PB 10506): Serrations were machined into the mating faces of the con rod and the big-end cap, which gave a stronger and more accurate location.

Brakes (from E0 PB 10594 and E0 SA 56R): A fully hydraulic footbrake system (from Girling) was introduced, a major engineering change. The previous (Girling hydro mechanical) system employed a floating tension-type master cylinder that operated the front leading/trailing shoes hydraulically, and the (mechanical) rod and cable handbrake system to the rear. This was supposed to give confidence to those customers who were reared on rod brakes, that in the event of hydraulic failure they would not be left without braking. The revised system resulted in all four wheels being hydraulically braked, with the handbrake a quite separate system. In addition the brake lining area was increased, and the front units now enjoyed twin leading shoes (wherein the leading edge of the shoes is pushed by the wheel cylinder against the hub). This is sometimes known as 'self-servo', because the action means that the rotation of the hub causes the lining contact pressure to be greater. The effect of this change meant that several associated alterations were required. For instance, all four brake hubs and back plates were redesigned; a revised (longer) rear axle was required, along with a different propshaft and transverse stay (Panhard rod); and the handbrake arrangement was totally altered, along with the master cylinder. This upgrade was expensive for the company to introduce, but well worth the effort, as braking performance improved significantly as a result.

Model change (from E0 PB to E0 PC): The 1951 model Javelins appeared from October 1950. Headlights increased in diameter from 5.25in to 7in (13 to 17cm).

Wooden dashboard styling as fitted to the first of the Javelin de Luxe models in 1950. (Geoff McAuley)

The 'standard' Javelin Saloon managed with the previous year's metal dashboard, but was now bereft of armrests. Seat facing material was subsequently replaced with a hard-wearing PVC (that, ironically, proved to be more durable than the leather). The price of both cars was reduced from the previous version, the basic price of the Saloon de Luxe being £695, and the Saloon £595. The earlier model had been priced at £738 basic in 1949.

Even the Saloon was quite well appointed, and was some way removed from Palmer's original idea of the car being utilitarian. Indeed, he was never overwhelmingly enthusiastic about the de Luxe's adoption of a wooden dashboard.

Solid tappets (cam followers) (from E0 PC 11907): The American-derived 'Zero-lash' hydraulic tappets had proved to be prone to mis-operation through contamination, and were also costly and sometimes difficult to obtain. A simpler, solid type was introduced, along with associated changes to the camshaft and pushrods. Most engines running today employ solid tappets. As far as is known, most Jupiters were shipped with solid-tappet engines.

Tyre size (de Luxe models from Feb 1951): The tyre size for the de Luxe Javelins was increased from 5.25-16in to 5.50-16in, the Jupiter tyre size.

Javelin radiator grill (from E0 PC 15631): A two-piece cast aluminium grille finished in satin silver lacquer replaced the one-piece chromed brass strip version. A new bonnet badge and revised centre chrome strip were also fitted; this gave a rather stronger appearance to the front of the car, though it was slightly less convenient to use, since the lower portion required the application of a long screwdriver to operate the 'Dzus'-type securing clips.

Oil filter assembly (from E1 PC 16603): The original Vokes type filters were replaced with the more common Tecalamit type. This was accompanied by revisions to the mounting casting (the so-called rear timing cover), which now incorporated a bypass valve to ensure continuance of oil flow should the filter element become blocked.

Water pump (from E1 PC 18140): An improved water pump and fan assembly were fitted. The fan became a single pressing with a modified taper for easier removal, and a slip ring 'shroud' was affixed to the pump impeller to increase flow.

Gearbox: The ultimately successful attempt to replace the Meadows-built gearbox (as fitted to Javelins from the start) with Jowett-built gearboxes, is chronicled in Chapter 11. It is thought that virtually all Jupiters were fitted with the Jowett box from new. The opportunity was taken to alter the gearing so that the intermediates were of lower ratio (i.e. higher geared) than before. Top gear remained the same at 1:1. Meadows gearboxes are serial numbered 50000 to at least 66485. Jowett-built gearboxes can be identified by the prefix 'J' on the serial number and run from J1 to at least J9437. Of course this does not mean that 25,922 Javelins and Jupiters were built!

Electric fuel pump (Jupiter only) (from E1 SA 439): A revised SU fuel pump with increased flow was fitted, and its position was changed from the bulkhead to the underside of the chassis on the right-hand side. This eliminated fuel starvation during hot-weather driving. An under-floor, glass bowl-type filter was also introduced. From E1 SA 504, the three-way fuel tap and reserve supply system was dispensed with.

Radiator (Jupiter only) (from E2 SA 458 LHD and E2 SA 695 RHD): A revised radiator was fitted, with a larger matrix area and a bigger header tank. The overall height of the radiator was thereby increased.

Camshaft adjustment (from E1 PD 19295/ E1 SA 481): To achieve more accurate setting of the valve timing, a modified camshaft chainwheel was fitted, incorporating a stepped vernier utilizing a six-position dowel, allowing for adjustment accuracy of plus/minus 0.75 degree.

Air cleaners (Jupiter only) (from E2 SA 590): The bulkhead-mounted Vokes air filter (behind the radiator) was replaced by two AC wire-mesh types, one mounted on each carburettor. The Vokes type is now quite rare on Jupiters, but is still found. The New Zealand Jowett Car Club have produced an adaptation so that a modern filter insert can fit inside the original Vokes casing.

Oil cooler (Jupiter only: from E2 SA 631): The early chassis-mounted oil cooler in front of the radiator was replaced with an engine-mounted version. The oil temperature capillary tube was accordingly required to be longer than before. Due to shortages it may be that most new coolers went on export models.

Carburettors (Jupiter only) (from E2 SA 657): The Zenith type 30VIG5 (with accelerator pump) was replaced by the simpler 30VM (without accelerator pump).

Steering wheel (from E2 PD 20881): A revised 'clear-vision' steering wheel for de Luxe models had the spokes formed in an arrowhead shape, improving the view of the instruments, which were now surrounded with chrome bezels and housed in a differently styled wooden dashboard (de Luxe model). Whether or not the instruments could be read more easily is, how-ever, debatable. This steering wheel was now secured to the inner steering column by splines rather that a Woodruff key, which facilitated the centralization of its position in the 'straight-ahead' position.

Front suspension (from E2 PD 21868 and E2 SA 865): A completely new front suspension arrangement (designed by Roy Lunn) was introduced. This became known as the 'rubber-bushed' version. Many grease nipples were eliminated by replacing metal bushes with Metalastik rubber variants. Upper and lower wishbones, along with the swivel pins and dampers, were all different from the earlier version (although the early lower wishbone can be modified to take the later suspension). The torsion bars, wheel hubs, backplates and brake components all remained unaltered.

Crankcase oil flow (from E2 PD 21937 and E2 SA 882): Various oilways within the cylinder block, the filter housing and the oil pump were increased in diameter, and other minor internal oil-related changes were made. This modification can most easily be identified by the larger diameter oil bypass pipe that connects externally to the filter housing.

For the 1952 Javelin de Luxe model the dashboard was modernized, but the visibility of the gauges was not quite as good as before. (Geoff McAuley)

Crankshaft and cylinder block (from E2 PD 22190, but including several earlier numbers, and E2 SA 882): The so-called Series III crankshaft (not to be confused with the oval web type) had minor changes to the oilways and the grinding profile of the radii at the crankpin edges, but is most easily identified by the presence of ¹⁵/₁₆in (0.9375mm) holes bored horizontally through the crankpins. (A few early versions had the former modifications but were without the bored crankpins.) This crankshaft proved to be quite durable, but occasional breakages are not unknown.

From this time the crankcases were cast with radial stiffening ribs radiating from the area of the main bearing housings. These blocks also enjoyed larger oilways for the improved flow of lubricant.

Soon after the introduction of the above modifications, the cylinder blocks were stamped with

Strengthening ribs and larger oilways on the Series III cylinder block. Note the repaired frost damage, not uncommon on Javelin/Jupiter engines. (Geoff McAuley)

The Javelin for 1954 would have had this dashboard. The control on the extreme right is a new horn button, as for the R4. Move it to any position to operate. (Woods Visual Imaging)

the letters PE (Javelin engines). Some blocks also displayed the number 3 stamped on the upper face adjacent to the filter housing. Series III Jupiter engines sometimes had the letter 'G' stamped on them.

Oil pump (from E2 PE 23122 and E2 SC 945): An improved oil pump was fitted that had a longer body, thus being fully submerged in the sump and ensuring instant self-priming. An adjustable oil-pressure relief valve was also incorporated. The pump gear dimensions and therefore the pumping rate were unchanged.

Camshaft (from E2 PE 23643 and E2 SC 957): The front end of the camshaft was fitted with an extension peg that provided a bearing surface. The front timing cover was also fitted with a screwed thrust peg that aligned with the camshaft. The lateral position of the adjustable peg could be altered and was secured by a locknut, thus containing camshaft endfloat; this replaced the previous spring-loaded arrangement, and eliminated an occasional annoying knocking sound. It was subsequently retro-applied to many earlier engines.

Crankcase (from E3 PE 24111). The so-called 'rubber liner seal' or 'O-ring liner' crankcases were introduced; these used a modified liner and block, enabling metal-to-metal contact between liner and block. Sealing was effected with a small-section neoprene 'O' ring that sat in a chamfer between the liner and the block. The change ensured constant 'nip' of the cylinder-head gaskets, and thus eliminated the possibility of liner sinkage.

This was effectively the final version of the Javelin/Jupiter engine. Following extensive continuous testing at the Motor Industry Research Association's new test track, it was shown to be extremely durable.

Much of the above development work was executed under the direction of the indefatigable Horace Grimley, whom, it can safely be recorded, played a greater role than anyone in keeping the Javelin ahead of its competitors during a production life of more than six years. But the fact that a 1947 Javelin looked, sounded and went much the same as a 1953 model is ample testament to the genius of Palmer's original design.

9 Life After Palmer

By the end of the 1940s the Javelin was well established and greatly admired; agencies had been set up around the world, and the government's call to export had been answered with vigour. However, 1949 had been a rather seminal year for Jowett, the departure of Palmer and Callcott Reilly seeming to have had an indefinable but unsettling effect on the company. True, attentions were now diverted by the Jupiter project, and Palmer's job was filled by another outstanding designer, Roy Lunn, who joined from Aston Martin. Lunn was to figure prominently in the design of the CD range of vehicles and the Jupiter R4. He subsequently went to Ford UK, Ford USA and American Motors.

There was now great pressure to reduce costs and to pitch the Javelin into a less expensive market segment. The 1950 models (announced in October 1949) offered the option of a de Luxe version with smarter interior and a wooden dashboard; they were advertised at £695 basic price for the de Luxe, and £595 basic for the saloon, the latter sometimes unofficially being referred to as the 'standard' Javelin.

Senior managers were implored to make economies, one of which subsequently materialized as a decision to manufacture gearboxes 'in house'; the significance of this is considered in Chapter 11. On the whole, however, the company's finances were improving, and the sporting achievements of the Javelin were now being reinforced by the Jupiter. Rallying successes were particularly important because, unlike today, competing cars were quite close in specification to those that could be bought in the showroom – indeed, some event organizers penalized any car that was not completely standard. So people would identify with sporting success because,

Tea all round for competitors of the 1951 Monte Carlo Rally. This is Jimmy Blumer's car. (Photo-Plage)

Roy Lunn

Royston Charles Lunn AMIMechE was born on 26 June 1925 at Richmond, in Surrey. Educated at Kingston Technical College, he studied engineering and then served an apprenticeship as a toolmaker with HEM Engineering Ltd from 1939–43.

After gaining a Higher National Certificate in mechanical engineering, Roy Lunn joined the Royal Air Force, transferring to RAF Farnborough where he was engaged on engine design work until being demobilized in 1946. He then joined AC Cars as a draughtsman/designer, and worked on new models. In 1947 he joined Aston Martin Lagonda Ltd, becoming assistant to Claude Hill, then Aston's chief designer.

Lunn was appointed by Jowett Cars Ltd as chief designer in 1949, where he developed suspension modifications to current cars. He was heavily involved in the design of the new CD range and the R4 Jupiter.

From January 1954, he joined the Ford Motor Co. Ltd at Birmingham, to help set up their vehicle research department (where he took on a handful of craftsmen from Jowett's experimental section), initially working on the Anglia 105E concept. From there he became car product planning manager at Dagenham, and subsequently transferred to Ford Motor Co. USA, being put in charge of advanced concepts, and taking design responsibilities for the then new Mustang project. He eventually became involved in developing the Ford GT40 into a Le Mans winner and Ferrari beater. In 1971 he joined American Motors, heading up development of the Jeep brand, and engineering the Cherokee and CJ-7 models. He then went on to head the design of the innovative AMC Eagle four-wheel-drive car, a concept that might now be known as a 'sports utility vehicle', much copied by manufacturers worldwide.

One of the motor industry's cleverest and most prolific designers, Roy Lunn was an excellent choice to succeed Gerald Palmer. Unfortunately, Jowett's demise meant that the Bradford company did not benefit significantly from his great potential.

Lunn, who is married to Jeanie and has two daughters, is now retired and resides in Florida, USA.

quite literally, the car they might buy or own was capable of winning – in the right hands!

Reliability was constantly being improved, although things weren't quite so rosy in mainland Europe, particularly in mountainous regions where extended climbs could result in overheated engines. However, improvements were made to the radiator, cylinder heads and thermostat, all of which helped. The addition of a radiator-mounted oil cooler for export cars in 1951 (also fitted to some home models) gave additional relief on continental mountain passes.

Myriad small changes were made in the cause of development, Horace Grimley and his small team working tirelessly to improve the package. For 1952 the de Luxe model was offered with yet another wooden dashboard design, a little more modern than before, with chrome surrounds to the gauges. Little else was changed on the car until the arrival of Roy Lunn's rubber-bushed suspension for the PE model range, also incorporated on late PD models from July 1952. The car was now pretty well at the end of its development.

By this time, however, production delays caused by gearbox maladies (see Chapter 11) were probably beginning to affect sales. New cars of other makes were generally rather easier to get hold of now, and potential customers were not prepared to wait for an indeterminate period. Jowett seems to have managed to keep the lid on the reasons for delayed deliveries, but unfinished cars were now collecting around the factory and in other locations. The flow of bodies from Briggs continued unabated, and these had to be paid for, but revenues were diminishing. A major crisis was unfolding.

In the 1950s Javelin competition successes continued, and were reinforced with others by its stable-mate the Jupiter.

The International RAC Rally of Great Britain

In 1952 came an impressive performance from Marcel Becquart and Roy Lunn in a factory-entered car in the International RAC Rally of

Over 200 Javelins parked around the factory during the time of the gearbox problems. A group of four pitched roofs covers the experimental department. (Woods Visual Imaging)

Great Britain. Becquart had intended entering his Farina Jupiter, but the car was rejected as non-standard, contrary to normal European practice where the definition of a 'standard car' applied to chassis and engine only. Becquart therefore had to resort to the factory competition Javelin HAK 743 that he first drove as late as the Sunday afternoon before the Monday start.

This RAC was a controversial event, with a number of unpopular administrative decisions taken by the organizers. The Silverstone test was cancelled owing to bad weather, and this resulted

International RAC Rally 1952. Storming run by Becquart at Scarborough's Oliver's Mount took the Javelin to victory in both closed car categories. (JCC)

Becquart's menu card with the signatures of Bert Hadley, Pat and Tommy Wise and Mike Wilson. (Becquart)

in the last test at Scarborough's Oliver's Mount taking on a disproportionate significance in the overall results. Becquart, however, lying fifth place in class as the cars drew into Scarborough, knew that an all-out attempt here was required of him. He drove like a man possessed, displaying great speed and regularity, and thereby brought the Javelin home to lead not only its class, but also the closed car category of all capacities.

Much praise was heaped on Becquart during the prize-giving celebrations later that evening, during which Morgan co-driver Jackie Reece publicly praised the Jowett driver for going like 'sh★t off a shovel!'. Becquart is reported to have given Reece a puzzled look, and with a twinkling eye and in a fake broken English accent mischievously enquired, 'Please, what eez a shovel?'

The Best Ladies' award also went to a Javelin crew, Mrs 'Billy' Mitchell and Mrs Lola Grounds.

Jollity at the 1952 RAC prize-giving. Left to right: Goff Imhoff, Ann Hall, Marcel Becquart. (Collection Joves)

The National Fuel Economy Run

By complete contrast, in the following August, motoring journalist and broadcaster Gordon Wilkins entered Javelin HAK 743 (Becquart's RAC Rally winning car) in the *News Chronicle*'s first National Fuel Economy Run. This comprised an 828-mile (1,332km) run on public roads through Wales, the Midlands, North Yorkshire, Lancashire and then into Edinburgh. The sometimes mountainous route was far from easy, and involved a good mix of commuters, sheep, 'aggressive' A1 drivers and variable weather conditions. In order to try to give a fair chance to different categories of car, a rather complex formula was used whereby credit or debit mpg handicaps were applied, depending on the standing quarter-mile acceleration of the cars (as per *The Autocar* road tests), and also the interior dimensions. Curiously, a car with thickly padded seats was less advantageously handicapped than a similar model with thinner seats (as might be found with de luxe or standard versions of the same basic car).

Wilkins had long taken an interest in fuel economy issues, even though the subject might not have been at the forefront of his mind when he was racing the R1 Jupiter at Le Mans! As is the case 50 years on, petrol in Britain was heavily taxed, and was the subject of much grumbling debate. Wilkins knew that attention to every small detail was the route to extreme fuel efficiency. He inflated the Javelin's tyres to 60psi, but proclaimed that comfort was such that it was still '... possible to sleep undisturbed on the back seat'. He does not, however, reveal whether this assertion was tested by the driver during the run! He realized that retention of heat in the engine was vital, and so completely blanked off the radiator grille. In reporting the event, he made reference to removing the cooling fan, filling the engine with SAE 10W oil, reducing the carburettor jet sizes and reducing the charging rate of the dynamo. He utilized a slightly raised compression ratio, but complained that this could not fully be exploited because of the low octane rating of 'pool' petrol.

'Free-wheeling' in neutral was permitted by the rules, and on some stretches Wilkins found that he could cruise for up to 50 per cent of the time. The three-day event involved 32 hours of 'extremely fatiguing' driving, at the conclusion of which the Javelin had achieved an actual overall average consumption of an astounding 67.86mpg (4.17ltr/100km), to win the event outright. A much-fancied Fiat 500 could only manage 57.5mpg (4.9ltr/100km).

The International Tulip Rallies 1952 and 1953

Fuel economy was far from the thoughts of the contestants of the fiercely fought International Tulip Rallies of 1952 and 1953.

The Dutch International Tulip Rally had started in 1949, but despite its name it covered large tracts of Europe and was to become a firm favourite on the rallying calendar. There were usually six or seven starting points in perhaps five countries (including the UK), with about 2,000 miles (3,200km) to be covered over often difficult terrain. Special tests at the end included circuit racing. In its first year there was just the one Javelin entry (that of Bill Robinson and Towers Leck), but it had an undistinguished result. The 1950 event attracted over 300 entries, five of which were Javelins – the highest placed was Bill Robinson's at class eleven. The following year again attracted more than 300 cars, but this time the Jowett tally had risen to fourteen. Robinson, now in a Jupiter, was the leading Jowett at seventh in the 1,500cc category, with a Javelin two places lower.

For the 1952 Tulip, a very resolute Dutchman, Count Hugo van Zuylen van Nijevelt, decided it was time his home rally was won by a Dutchman, preferably himself! With great determination he set about preparing his Javelin in a way that used interpretation of the rules to full effect. This even extended to replacing the rear doors with laminated board and perspex for lightness and better visibility. Pride was at stake, for a more famous Dutchman, Maurice Gatsonides, was also entered, in a factory-prepared Javelin. Van Nijevelt knew that keeping the engine at the correct temperature would be difficult, and so employed a full radiator muff – the Javelin with

*Mr and Mrs J. Thoenes and
D. Carter tackling Belgian
pavé on the International
Tulip Rally of 1953.
(J-Appert Reportage)*

the radiator behind the engine is prone to carburettor icing in cold, damp weather. Unfortunately, with a first place in prospect, he forgot to open the muff for the test at the Zandvoort racing circuit, and the car seriously overheated – and that was the end of his rally. Nevertheles, Javelins took second, fourth (Gatsonides), sixth, ninth and eleventh in their category.

For 1953 van Nijevelt came back more determined than ever and, with navigator F. M. A. Eschauzier, he joined eight other Javelins and a Jupiter. Although by now Jowett's Arthur Jopling had decided to cut back on works-entered competition, motoring journalists and other enthusiasts continued to extol the Javelin's virtues, and sporting Javelin owners were as keen as ever to contest competitive events. This time, mindful of the organizers' regulation that cars should be truly standard production, van Nijevelt's Javelin had four proper doors – but crucially, the radiator muff (held in place with press studs) could be opened from within the cockpit by pulling on a length of string! As mentioned, French rally ace Marcel Becquart had persuaded Jowett to lend him a works Javelin. Following his spectacular result in the RAC Rally the previous year, Jopling decided that the cost would be justified, and a 'very lively' Javelin was prepared specially for him. Alas, the car was faster than it ought to have been, sporting as it did a Jupiter exhaust pipe and probably other non-standard components as well. Despite 'winning' the class, Becquart was disqualified, much to his extreme embarrassment and annoyance. He was never again to drive for Jowett.

Several other leading cars were also disqualified for technical infringements, and because the overall results were based on a 'class improvement' system, van Nijevelt found himself not only class winner, but also the overall winner of the event! J. Scheffer and G. J. Willing's Javelin came second in class, with O. E. Homan and R. S. de Boer finishing third; so Jowett also won the one-make team prize. The Jupiter, this year in another category, finished class fourth. Notably all these Jowetts were Dutch entries.

Six years on from its introduction, then, a standard privately prepared Javelin was still capable of winning international rallies – outright. The

Van Nijevelt chases Becquart at Zandvoort, 1953 International Tulip Rally. (J-Appert Reportage)

1953 Tulip had produced an amazing result for Javelins. For a car nearing the end of its production life, this victory in an international rally was a fine achievement, and further testament to the pace and durability of its design.

Following the 1952 Motor Show, Grandfield organized an extended trial for three Javelins and three Jupiters at the Motor Industries Research Association (MIRA) test site in Warwickshire. The facility was still under construction, and the drivers therefore had to negotiate a triangular circuit marked out by oildrums. 'Operation Boomtown' was the nickname given to this amazing exercise, and more can be read about this in Chapter 11.

These tests validated the integrity of the Series III cars, although strangely, and despite falling sales, the company did not make public this reliability marathon. This was most unusual for Jowett, who traditionally took great delight in vaunting its performance achievements in full page advertisements. Perhaps it was thought that it would be tantamount to admitting to pre-existing reliability problems, and the data therefore reserved just for convincing those who raised the issue.

Falling Sales

Sales of the Javelin during 1952 had been disappointing, having failed to reach the level of the previous year. Putting aside supply problems that may have resulted from the gearbox difficulties (again, see Chapter 11), an ever-widening choice of cars was now available to the British consumer, many of which were priced some way below the Jowett. In recognition of this, when in early 1953 the government reduced purchase tax on cars, the company reduced pre-tax prices. These cuts resulted in the models now being offered as follows:

Model	Old Price	New Price	Total (with PT)
Javelin	£695	£625	£886.55
Javelin de Luxe	£775	£675	£957.40
Jupiter Mk 1A	£895	£795	£1,127.40

The Jupiter price was further reduced in October, at which time a brief but significant press

A cigarette calms the nerves of this Jowett driver on the regularity run, 1953 International Monte Carlo Rally. (JCC)

1952 International Lisbon Rally. Nancy Mitchell and Joyce Leavens on their way to winning the Coupe des Dames. (JCC)

*1954 Monte. Even after the
end of production, Jowetts
continued to compete. (JCC)*

announcement was made that 'Production of bodies for the Javelin has been held up'

Alas, these price cuts alone failed to revive sales to their 1949–51 levels. For all sorts of reasons, some discussed elsewhere, 1953 was a bad period for Jowett. A Javelin advertisement placed in *The Autocar* in April 1953 declared, 'Not for everyone this extra touch of class; not for everyone this extra comfort and safety and liveliness …'. Prophetic words indeed: would that the company could have claimed otherwise.

In Chapter 12 we examine the circumstances surrounding the cessation of supplies from Briggs. It is a sad irony that, at the very time when the Javelin was technically at its best, a situation arose whereby the car could no longer be built. We will see that a replacement was well advanced, but that a combination of events contrived to make continued production impossible. It is worth noting, however, that it was continuing to attract exemplary road-test comments in the motoring press, as well as being capable of winning major sporting events, just as it had done at the beginning of its production life. Perhaps the styling was now becoming somewhat dated, but there was little in

the technical design that would be surpassed for some years to come. Even in 1953 *The Motor* stated that the Javelin was 'still the fastest 1.5 litre saloon [we have] tested since the war'.

The Enigmatic Javelin

Owners continued to race and rally the Javelin even after production ceased; indeed, to this day the cars continue to be used in competition. There is probably not a single year since production began during which a Javelin has not competed in one way or another.

So how can we sum up this enigma of a motor car? In concept and design it was undoubtedly in a class apart from other mainstream vehicles of its time. Nothing about the design was particularly revolutionary in its own right, but a combination of cleverly thought-out features guaranteed an overall package that managed to combine conflicting requirements in a quite remarkable way. The car was comfortable, yet handled well for its time. It was roomy, but also economical, its streamlined shape belying the amount of luggage that could be stacked into the boot. It was well equipped. It would flatter a driver, but allow passengers to enjoy comparative luxury; perhaps most of all, it was desirable – it was the car to have for the non-conformist, the driver with a taste for adventure and an eye for good design.

Of course there were weaknesses. A car as adventurous as this, built by such an under-resourced company, was almost bound to have some engineering deficiencies. The engine would have benefited from more early development, and the complexity of the body meant that it would always be expensive to produce, thus taking it above a populous market segment that would have ensured higher sales. It is pertinent to note the success of the Standard Vanguard, Morris Oxford and Austin A40 for example, all technically inferior cars but far more successful than the Javelin within the harsh reality of the marketplace. When considering reliability issues however, we should not lose sight of the millions of modern cars that are recalled for attention to serious manufacturing and design faults, many of these from some of the world's largest manufacturers.

It is interesting to remind ourselves of Palmer's intention that the Javelin should be 'a world car'. Another fast-back world car with a flat-four engine, conceived by a certain Herr Hitler, had sold rather better, as the figures in the table indicate. If only these figures had been transposed!

The legacy, then, is a car that was not an

Year	Javelin bodies produced	VW Beetle sales
1947	31	8,973
1948	1,558	19,220
1949	5,450	46,594
1950	5,551	90,558
1951	5,769	105,482
1952	4,060	135,970

overwhelming sales success. History has been kind to the Javelin, however, and surely it can be fondly remembered alongside such luminaries as Citroën's Light 15 and DS models, Lancia's Aprilia, Appia and Fulvia, the NSU RO80, the Alfasud and Audi's A2. The criterion here is not necessarily one of marketing success. Rather, these cars and others of their type shine like beacons from the anonymity of 'bread-and-butter' models which, sadly but predictably, have long been the life-blood of the successful motor manufacturer.

So one begs the question, 'was the Javelin too good to succeed?' Well, there's no simple answer, but the fact that the question can reasonably be (and often is) asked, is perhaps in itself a fitting tribute to all those fine people who were associated with the creation and development of this extraordinary car.

10 The Jupiter in the USA

Sports car racing, rallying and hill-climbing re-started in the USA in the late 1940s. Fuelled by returning US servicemen and their experiences with European sports cars, battle was engaged between MG (over 10,000 were sold into the USA between 1947 and the end of 1951), Singer, Siata, OSCA, Porsche, Ferrari, Allard and the like, as well as home-gown creations based on all manner of material from the humble

Ashley Pace's SCCA badge. (Collection Joves)

Crosley to the mighty V8-engined Cunning-hams. Huge crowds would turn out to watch, giving these events an importance superior to better-documented races in, for example, Britain, where sometimes the crowd at national races would number a few thousand, with rather less in attendance at club races.

Early Events

Most of the early events took place in the North-Eastern US and were staged by the Sports Car Club of America (SCCA) - this club being a post-war outgrowth of the Automobile Racing Club of America - but by 1950 when the Jupiter hit the scene race meetings of various types were being staged by other groups as well, and some of the earlier venues had continued and had grown in popularity. These race meetings may have been held on private roads, municipal roads (sometimes a combination of both), fairgrounds or municipal airfields. The airfield races filled a gap following tragic accidents at some of the true road courses, so much so that for a couple for years starting in late 1952 hugely successful races were held on US Air Forces bases under the combined aegis of the SCCA and the Strategic Air Command. These races were well organized and safe, and attracted large crowds while the Strategic Air Command was able to raise money for its recreation fund for things that did not receive appropriations. Needless to say, during these early years the distinction between Stock and Modified cars was not always clear, but it was in the so-called stock class that the Jupiter had its chance to show what it could do.

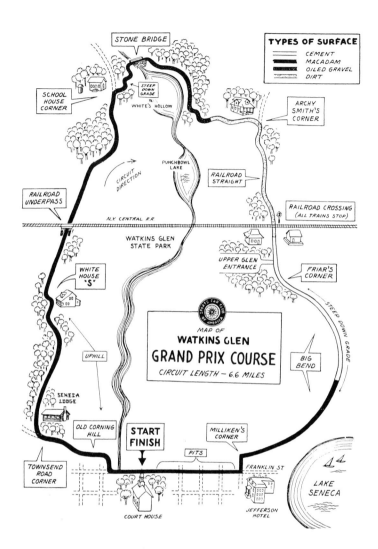

Watkins Glen circuit. Franklin Street occupies part of an old Indian trail, a reminder that this was once Seneca Indian territory. (SCCA)

Watkins Glen. For the Jupiter, American motor sport began inauspiciously in that most auspicious of surroundings - Watkins Glen. The circuit was formed, in those days, from streets and country lanes in and around the small town of that name on the southern tip of the Seneca Lake in upstate New York. The date was 23 September 1950, and it was reported that maybe 100,000 spectators had gathered. The second event of the day was for 1,500cc sports cars, an eight-lapper for the Queen Catharine Montour Cup. The driver was Lawrence Whiting Jr, and the car was the prototype Jupiter.

Earlier in the year Lawrence had come fifth racing a Simca Sport amongst MG TCs at an event on the Studebaker test circuit, and then won a ten-lap novice race in his TD around a country road circuit at Elkhart Lake, Wisconsin. How and why he came to be racing the very first Jupiter, the original USA show car, the genuine Jupiter number one, we will surely never know.

The race began with a Le Mans running start, with Whiting about half-way down the echelon. Soon a *Road and Track* photographer caught the stationary Jupiter, the nearside front pushed in somewhat, presumably after an encounter with a haybale, and Whiting getting out to check the damage. He restarted but after an otherwise undistinguished first few laps, the magazine reports that on lap five 'The Javelin Jupiter seems to be out of the race as sounds indicate all is not well with the engine.' Another report has it that the engine 'sounded sour from the start'. We hear no more of this particular car until it showed up in Wisconsin in 1968 with no bonnet and no engine, and with only 1,031 miles indicated on the odometer.

Giants Despair. Things went rather better for George Rand at the Giants Despair Hillclimb, in the foothills of the Ponoco Mountains, Pennsylvania, over 11–12 May 1951. In front of 5,000 spectators George, in a class of eighteen of which fourteen were MGs, ascended in 1m 32.3s, placing the Jupiter equal ninth with a TC.

Burke Mountain. At the Burke Mountain SCCA hillclimb on 24 June 1951, Dexter Coffin and his Jupiter ascended in the class-winning time of 4min 42.2s, respectively 22 and 35 seconds ahead of the next-placed Porsche and TD.

Thompson Speedway. There were two days of time trials, sprints and races at the Thompson Speedway, Connecticut, SCCA National Meet during 21-22 July 1951. In the flying half-mile test George Weaver set FTD in his blown Maserati. The Jupiters of Hugh Byfield and Dexter Coffin set disappointing standing quarter times of 24.0s and 24.1s, not surprisingly slower than nearly all the MGs, although fractionally quicker than a Simca 8. In the flying half-mile test Coffin's Jupiter was equal second in its class with a TD, just pipped by a TC. On Day Two races were held around a unique circuit, actually two concentric ovals sharing the same straightaway, with the cars starting on the straight, next to the grandstand. After almost a full lap on the inner track the cars wriggled their way through alternately two left-handers and two right-handers onto the outside half-mile banked circuit for four laps, then came back onto the inside for the final one. Drivers found these bends were

quite interesting, especially the left-handers. In the five-lap 1,500cc production sports car race Weaver, not only a fast driver but a careful one, now drove the stock Jupiter of his good friend Dexter Coffin. Hugh Byfield was forced to retire his Jupiter from this event but Weaver put on a splendid performance in the borrowed car to win ahead of several MGs.

Elkhart Lake. Two Jupiters attended the Elkhart Lake, Wisconsin, Rally and Day of Races and Tests on 26 August 1951. The organizers had the excellent idea of having a rally to their race meet with cars converging from all corners of the country. In a complicated formula that combined overall distance travelled, engine size and car's age, the Jupiter of G. B. Reed was placed tenth in the rally out twenty-six classified finishers, whilst in the novice race Hugh Byfield (Jupiter) was placed fifth in class at thirteenth overall, with three MGs and a Fiat above and a 2-litre Lea Francis (in another class) and two more MGs below. Larry Whiting was back with his MG in a senior race where he finished class fifth.

Watkins Glen. During the weekend of 14–15 September 1951 Jupiters returned to Watkins Glen for the fourth annual meeting. Here we have Hugh Byfield in his own Jupiter, and George Weaver in the ex-Le Mans R1 brought across from England by the East Coast importer Max Hoffman. Jowett's pride and joy was described by *Motor Trend* as 'this minor projectile of interesting bug-like outline'. Weaver had dominated the first race, the Seneca Cup, in his Maserati type V8R1 known as 'Poison Lil', and he set out to similarly dominate the eleven-lap Queen Catharine Montour Cup in the Jowett type R1.

Photographic evidence places the R1 between a third and half-way down the starting line-up, with perhaps a dozen cars in front. The Le Mans start sent the thirty-three drivers scampering for their cars – two MGs and a Siata Sport were the first away but by the end of the first lap Weaver had forced his way into the lead. The closest competition for him emerged as the Lester-MG of David

The bug-like R1 as prepared for the Le Mans of 1951. It ran in this form at Watkins Glen, painted white. (Woods Visual Imaging)

Viall which harried the flying Jowett for much of the race while never quite managing to summon up the power to get past; at the chequered flag after just over an hour's driving, thanks to a brief pitstop by Viall, almost two minutes separated them. An HRG took third spot, the Siata Sport fourth and the highest-placed MG fifth. Arguably this victory stands as the R1's greatest triumph.

Newton Small at Torrey Pines, December 1951. Note the plated trafficator slot, and the absence of louvres. (Ted Miller collection)

George Weaver, Watkins Glen 1951, two wins but three trophies. Left to right: Seneca Cup, Queen Catharine Montour Trophy (presented by the Montour Falls Chamber of Commerce) and the Queen Catharine Trophy (presented by the organizers). (Barbara Weaver)

Torrey Pines. It was not until the 9 December 1951 at Torrey Pines near San Diego in southern California that sports car fans witnessed the first West Coast race appearance of a Jupiter. The opening race meeting at this venue began with an event for 1,500cc stock sports cars. Newton Small's sweetly sounding Jowett soon worked its way into the lead and held it until the last lap when, in the excitement, its inexperienced driver got crossed up in a corner, spun into the straw and let a black TD past to push the Jupiter into second spot. Bruce Mooney, who himself later raced a Jupiter, came fourth in another TD.

Events Held in 1952

Vero Beach. Three races were held at Vero Beach, Florida, on 8 March 1952: a one-hour, a six-hour and a twelve-hour, the last two starting simultaneously. In the first, Bill Lloyd in his go-to-work Jupiter came third behind the glittering Glöckler-Porsche (a fully streamlined sports racer faster than XK120s and really in a class by itself in all respects including cost) driven by Max Hoffman, and an HRG, but ahead of numerous MGs, some supercharged. Bill commented after the race 'The Jupiter is a very nice little car, corners like a demon, is very comfortable, and stays up with the best of them.'

Although nominally third, this excellent unsung result has to be one of the best for Jowett Stateside. Of course it was an even better result for the HRG, a thirteen-year old car and a fifteen-year old design, with similar styling and discomforts to the MG.

Palm Springs. The opener at the Palm Springs Day of Road Races California on 23 March 1952 was for 1,500cc production cars. It was won easily by a Siata Sports, followed by a TDII, the Jupiter of Bruce Mooney, and another twelve finishers, mostly MGs. Another Jupiter, owned by Don Ricardo but driven by Englishman Dennis Buckley, sounded poorly and retired after three laps. The Jupiter of Terry Feil was also entered but it is not known how it fared, or even if it ran.

Bridgehamton. Under ideal weather conditions, spectacular road racing was on offer at Bridgehamton, New York, on 24 May 1952. There were almost 100 cars (divided into five classes) and a crowd estimated at 40,000 people, many of whom must have been bemused by some of the goings-on, as some drivers certainly were. Problems arose because Event 1 comprised two races run concurrently. It was for 1,500cc cars where the strictly stock group ran forty miles (64km - ten laps) for the Sagaponack Trophy while their modified brethren ran 100 miles (160km) for the Mecox Trophy. It took a full half-minute to get all thirty-two cars away. Richard Thierry was driving Bill Lloyd's strictly stock Jupiter as Lloyd was competing in an MG with an Offenhauser engine, while Hugh Byfield had also entered his Jupiter. Two Porsches immediately leaped ahead while Thierry followed by a Siata battled it out close behind. The Siata passed the Jupiter on lap 5, the positions reversed on the seventh, but on the eighth the Siata again passed the Jupiter and held its place to finish third with Thierry fourth, ahead of all the MGs; Siata and Jupiter raced on for a couple more laps but there was no further change. Byfield had a disappointing race, falling further and further behind to retire on lap nine. One Porsche and the Siata were originally in the modified group but were reclassified as stock - perhaps they were only a little modified! Quite a few Sagaponack cars, thanks to a dormant chequered flag, raced on for many more laps than their allotted ten.

Atlanta, Georgia. There was a tour to Mitch Werbell's Atlanta, Georgia, home on 21 June 1952, where three time trials took place.

These were (1) Standing Quarter Mile, (2) Flying Quarter with 360-degree turn midway, and (3) Timed Quarter with navigator holding an egg in a spoon at arm's length out of the window. The up-to-1,500cc class overall winner was Earle Yancey (Jupiter).

Results from FCCA Events. The Four Cylinder Club of America (FCCA) also promoted motor sport in those days. Here is a selection of results from some of their events. The second annual Scotchman's Drag Rally was on a day in June 1952. It was a three-hour jolly ending in Santa Barbara with Don Broderick (Jupiter) winning his class. In the Ivey Oil Rally on 20 July 1952 the same car and driver took the Sports Car class trophy in spite of the opening of the escape kit. On a day in August 1952 the Santa Barbara Rally attracted sixty-two entrants including the Jupiters of Hunter Hackney, Mel Allen and William Cochrane, who finished thirteenth, seventeenth and fiftieth respectively. William Cochrane was then the editor of the FCCA newsletter, Hackney was a law student. The Rally of a Thousand Curves 29 June 1952 was won outright by Hunter Hackney with Tom Ingram navigating. The much more ambitious Lake Tahoe Tally took place over a long weekend in August 1952. The route included dirt-roads, forests, steep grades (in one stage the cars climbed from 6,000ft to over 8,000ft in 25 minutes), potholed roads long in need of repair, mountain hairpins and desert; the last leg was taken flat out and resembled a road race. The third day was given over to a gymkhana. Hunter Hackney (Jupiter) with navigator John Orlando won the road section outright and tied second in the gymkhana, placing the Jupiter overall first with MGs taking the next three places. Hackney became the FCCA in Southern California Rally Champion for 1953.

Turner Air Force Base. At the Turner AFB, Albany, Georgia, Day of Races, on 26 October 1952, there were two Jupiters (for Ashley Pace and Frank Manley) amongst over eighty participants, of which thirty were in the Jupiter's class. In the Keenan Sowega Trophy Race (over fifty miles) for modified and unmodified 1,500cc production sports cars, Ashley Pace won a nice silver trophy for first in the unmodified class ahead of nine MGs, a Siata, a Porsche and a Crosley, with Manley somewhere in between.

Torrey Pines. Two Jupiters took part in the Torrey Pines Midwinter Races, California, 14 December 1952. Proceedings began with an event for novice drivers in two groups: cars of up to and over 1,500cc. Hunter Hackney in his first race won his class ahead of a Crosley and a TD, while Jim Lambros in another Jupiter spun off on the fast bend at the end of the pit straight, although he did return to the fray after the excitement had died down.

Hunter Hackney with the class-winner's trophy, Torrey Pines 1952. (Ted Miller collection)

Cal Marks (left) and Hunter Hackney, outside the World Wide Import Inc premises. The Jupiters are prepared for the Pebble Beach weekend of races, 18–19 April 1953. Marks chalked up a seventh and an eighth in races that included several specials. (Ted Miller collection)

Events Held in 1953

Bergstrom Air Force Base. On 12 April 1953 the Bergstrom AFB, Texas, attracted 35,000 spectators. In the third race, for modified and production 1,500cc sports cars, G. Wright (Jupiter) finished third behind a Porsche and a TD. Since the Jupiter was 6mph and 3mph (10km/h and 5km/h) respectively faster than the TD through the two speed traps, one can only suppose that the Jupiter's challenge to the MG must have faded towards the end of the race.

Phoenix. A weekend of races was staged at Phoenix Arizona over 2–3 May 1953. There were Porsches present, but presumably not the Super variant as they didn't do much. In the first race (eight laps) Hunter Hackney spun his Jupiter out of the lead on lap six but fought back to second at the flag behind a Singer; Cal Marks in the other Jupiter settled for third place. In the fifth race, for novices all classes, Cal Marks took class second. In the seventh race, for the Governor's Cup all classes, Hackney took first and Marks second in their category to cap an excellent weekend's racing for the Yorkshire cars.

Bridgehamton. Police estimated that 50,000 spectators came to Bridgehamton, NY, on 23 May 1953 to watch what was the fifth such event and the last on public roads following an accident that injured four spectators. The entry list for the Sagaponack Trophy this year comprised eight TDs, two Singers, six Porsches and the grey Jupiter of Pat Reidel. With the writing definitely on the wall for the 1,500cc English sports cars, the Jupiter took the chequered flag sixth behind the five finishing German cars.

Brooklyn. At the Floyd Bennett Field, a naval airbase at Sheepshead Bay, Brooklyn, a 4.3-mile (6.9km) circuit had been formed from macadam approach roads and concrete runways. On 29 August 1953 about 50,000 spectators gathered in the 110°F heat to watch the Sheepshead Trophy Race. A formula had been found to shut out Porsche: a ten-lap race was held for unmodified 1,500cc sports cars retailing for less than $3,000! The June 1951 price for the basic TD was $1,595 with the 60bhp TDII something over $2,000; the Jupiter sneaked through at $2,850 (New York price). The Porsche to race was the Super at a cost of about $4,000.

When racing got under way, a twin carburettor Singer took an immediate lead, at one stage thirty car lengths ahead of the Jupiter of Bill Lloyd (interestingly a Mk1a and therefore his second Jupiter), itself followed by twenty-seven

Jerry Van Vort

This is the story of Jerry Van Vort and his Jupiter, as told to Dave Burrows:

I bought my Jupiter in June 1952 after seeing one race at Lime Rock. It was from the first batch of Jupiters to come into the USA – the original owner was in banking circles in New Jersey. I used the Jupiter every day, as well as racing it at every possible chance. Under the best of conditions I was able to attain a top speed of 92mph (148km/h), while under race conditions normal top speeds were closer to 83mph (134km/h). From 1952 to 1957 I raced the Jupiter at least a half dozen times in club races on Long Island, at Lime Rock and Bridgehampton.

The Jupiter was a fun automobile and relatively easy to drive. I was at a disadvantage with the long shift pattern, but the car was easy to shift, and the transmission and clutch were dependable. The Jowett factory was extremely co-operative, and supplied any racing Jupiter with information and assistance. I removed the windscreen and used a small Brooklands aero screen, I cleaned the intake and exhaust ports, and did a valve job after every race to get absolute top performance out of the Jupiter. We never did a race without blowing the bottom end bearings. The big-end shells would show thirty odd cracks over the bearing face, although it never lost pressure. The engine was quite willing, and we would crank up to 7,000rpm in every gear. I never had crankshaft problems. I was told by Mil Kittler, president of Holley Carburettors, that the bearing problem was one of metallurgy, with English makers somewhat behind the USA in development. I kept torsion bars, bearings and shocks on hand. We did install thin head gaskets and special factory-supplied head studs, increasing the compression ratio.

Hoffman was the original distributor for the Jupiter in the New York area; initially I received a great deal of help with racing modifications from a Mr Grasso, Hoffman's top mechanic, and later from Major Seddon who assumed distribution when Hoffman dropped the Jupiter.

I do remember that no matter where I went with the Jupiter, it attracted a lot of attention. Jowetts were always considered a weird auto because of the engine configuration, and mechanics hated to work on them because torquing down the heads was critical. I loved the instrument panel since the instruments were accessible once the fascia was removed. I never won a race, but racing the Jupiter was exciting, and was also a social activity, and we met many delightful people and endured innumerable parties – difficult work, but someone had to do it!

The Jupiter was delightful to drive. You could set up a four-wheel drift easily and go floating round very nicely. Unfortunately the rear end could break loose – I lost it once on a 180-degree turn and bashed the rear and front fender as I went through the hay bales. This was my only mishap, and a chap in the Bronx took in the Jupiter and fixed the aluminium panelling.

I raced in the 1,500cc class and would always be beaten by the Porsches. The Jupiter did corner tightly and was really spectacular with stiffer shocks at the rear. It didn't have a hot engine, but it had a lot of 'get up and go' in second and third gear; its top speed wasn't great either, but it accelerated and cornered well.

I sold my Jupiter in 1957, and wasn't to drive another one for forty years – until an opportunity came to drive Dave Burrows' Jupiter at a Pittsburgh Vintage Grand Prix.

MGs. Showing great determination, Lloyd began to close the gap but, before he could overtake, the Singer was forced out with fading oil pressure, conceding victory to the Jupiter which finished well ahead of five TDs and the rest of the MGs.

Moffett Naval Airfield. The second race of the day at the Moffett Naval Airfield, California, on 16 August 1953, was for the Navcad Trophy. The Jowett Jupiter of Don Connelly was placed fifth in a class of twenty-three, ahead of seventeen

MGs. He was headed by a Simca, an MG special and two Porsches.

Madera. The Madera Road Races, central California, were held on a day in October 1953. The first race, for novice drivers, attracted a large field of TCs, TDs, some Porsches, a DB, and a white Jupiter special, which had had its engine somehow repositioned behind the front suspension. In this improbable vehicle Bud Grosso took an immediate lead but he was unable to hold on against repeated challenges from a TC as the Jupiter began to show signs of ignition bothers. It retired after three laps.

In the fourth race - thirty laps for senior drivers - Bill Behel now took the wheel of the Jupiter special, its ignition problems sorted. The Jupiter's new engine position had destroyed the car's normal good handling and Behel was completely foxed by the back end trying so hard to beat the front end round every corner. Eventually he had to retire the car for more work on the steering geometry.

Nothing more has ever been heard of this curious machine, unless perhaps it was the same Jupiter special that appeared at March Air Force Base on 7 November 1954. Whatever it was took third spot in a Junior race, behind an OSCA and an MG Special, but ahead of a Porsche and a Moretti.

Riverside. A reported 70,000 spectators came to the March AFB, Riverside, California on 8 November 1953. There were four races that day, three with Jupiters; Bill Behel was now racing an MG. Race 1: Jack Carberry (Jupiter) won his class convincingly ahead of the Jupiter of Joseph Weissman (in his very first race), a Porsche, a Siata

and a Singer. MGs ran in their own class but all finished behind Carberry. Race 2: Cal Marks (Jupiter) came in class second behind a Porsche but ahead of a Singer, an MG TDII, and the Jupiter of Jack Carberry. Race 3: Jack Carberry took the class leading an MG TD, with Cal Marks relegated to third. Thus ended a very good day for the Jupiter, and, one might say, taking into account the number of spectators, its last best day of racing anywhere.

Willow Springs. We end this by no means complete survey with a mention of the Willow Springs Hill Climb 13 December 1953, one hundred miles north of Los Angeles. A class win was recorded by a Jupiter.

In Summary

In its brief production life 252 Jupiters went to the USA with almost two thirds being sold by the West Coast distributor Angell Motors; compare this with 23,000 TDs between 1949 and 1953. Even in 1953 the MG was the USA's largest foreign car import. Angell Motors provided support for Jupiter racing men, as indeed did the Jowett factory which on more than one occasion

The six trophies earned by Cal Marks in one season's Jupiter racing. (Ted Miller collection)

shipped an engine to the USA gratis. The successes of Cal Marks were helped by the efforts of World Wide Import Inc, who took over Jupiter franchise following Angell's bankruptcy sometime late in 1952.

In the March 1953 edition of *Road and Track* the road test of Hunter Hackney's Jupiter was headed 'A thorough test of the Jupiter reveals a sturdy, fast, manueverable 1500cc sports car' and it went on:

> Needing little more than 15 seconds to attain the 60mph mark, and having the ability to record gratifyingly high pulling-power figures

on the Tapley meter, it would seem that the Jupiter could have done other than trail behind the 1,500cc competition in the past two years of West Coast racing.

The magazine concluded that the Jupiter:

> ... has handling qualities to satisfy nearly everyone – it will corner rapidly, safely, and certainly cannot be classed with family sedans. Its 0–60 performance (15.1 seconds) is definitely better than average and a genuine 90mph may be had under favourable conditions. It provided comfort and attractive appearance ...

11 Crankshafts, Gaskets, Gearboxes

The Javelin had emerged as a comfortable, brisk family saloon giving 75/80mph (120/129km/h) at 28/32mpg (10–8.8ltr/100km). Its power unit was rated at 52.5bhp at 4,500rpm. Early developments of the Javelin engine centred around bearing life and oiling – the flat-four layout contributed to higher oil temperatures, and under long-distance touring conditions a tendency to big-end and main-bearing failures was experienced. Part of the solution to this was to change the bearing material from white metal to a copper-lead alloy with an indium flash; initially this was just the big-end bearings, but soon the front and centre main bearings were changed as well

(the rear main, which incorporated the end-thrust surfaces, remained white metal). This change took place around the middle of 1949 when approximately 4,000 or so Javelins had been delivered. The new bearing material was harder and less forgiving than white metal, and before long it was found that the crank bearing surfaces had a short life, so induction-hardening of these surfaces was carried out. It also happened that crankshaft manufacture, initially by an outside sub-contractor, had at some stage been brought in-house, as it was company policy for Jowett to manufacture as much as possible themselves. Experiments were carried out to perfect

Tom Blackburn racing at Snetterton in July 1953. The crank broke the following year. (Ferret Fotographics)

the hardening technique, and the first hardened crank was introduced in May 1950 approximately. Whether or not the 1950 Le Mans Jupiter ran on a hardened shaft is not known, but it is probable, since these technical changes, as well as the Le Mans engines themselves, came from the experimental department.

Problems with Crankshaft Breakages

In time crankshafts began to break in service. Possibly the first – and certainly the first recorded instance of such a breakage – was in the RAC-TT International sports car race of September 1950. It was during this event of nearly 4 hours duration that, embarrassingly, the ex-Le Mans Jupiter broke its crank after having built up an impregnable class lead over the works MG TDs. Initially it was thought that this was a racing phenomenon confined to the Jupiter, for several did break in competition: Robinson broke one at Goodwood on 22 March 1952, while Tom Blackburn experienced the same failure during the 1954 Morecambe Rally. His Jupiter's engine had high compression pistons fitted, while Tom himself was a hard driver in those days. But it was undoubtedly a serious matter: two British Jupiter owners have reported that they broke not one, but two cranks during the first 18 months of ownership.

The 1950 TT Jupiter's engine was running at a compression ratio (cr) of 8.75:1 – Javelins ran at 7.2 and the standard Jupiter at 7.6 at this point in time. The problem only began to be addressed after cranks started breaking in the USA (where the cr was set to 8:0 and high touring speeds could be, and were, sustained for much longer periods than in the UK). Nevertheless it was not long before British and other Jupiters were similarly afflicted. An owner wrote:

When my Jupiter had covered about 22,000 miles suddenly there was a loud drumming sound for about four miles, followed by a very loud crashing noise. I free-wheeled into a garage, opened the bonnet, and when the engine ran it made an incredible noise. We saw that the front pulley was not running true, and concluded that the crank had broken. After the engine was rebuilt I was not allowed to keep the broken shaft on the grounds it wouldn't do Jowetts any good!

This unfortunate owner had a second crank fail at about 44,000 miles, but by then a much stronger component was available.

Keighley Laboratories, situated conveniently only a dozen miles from Idle, were frequently consulted by Jowett when technical problems loomed – the firm had been founded by Stephen Poole's elder brother William in the early 1920s to provide the motor industry with technical advice and guidance, and a group of very well qualified scientists worked there. A conventional crankshaft analysis was carried out. In this analysis only rotational and reciprocating masses were considered, and initial calculations showed that the crank should not fail. From inspection it was thought that the cranks were failing in bending, not torsion. Keighley Labs' explanation was that the crankcase was insufficiently stiff to resist combustion pressure loads (gas loads). They pointed out that aluminium alloy has only a third of the stiffness of the same section of cast iron, and also that the cranks were machined from cast blanks rather than forgings: with a forged crank the metal grain runs round the bends in the crank, making a stronger component. They went on to predict that Jowett would in time be inundated with broken cranks. As a result of this, from about March 1952, radial stiffening webs were added to the crankcase castings in the region of the main bearing housings, and together with the final oilway modifications, these changes were certainly incorporated by about the following June. It is worth pointing out that the first 2,000 or so engines were made from sand castings rather than gravity die castings. These earlier crankcases were heavier and presumably more rigid, which again may have contributed to a reduced tendency to crank breakage.

There was an inherent problem with crank manufacture in those days: the raw billets were produced by the open hearth process. This

The insides of a 1952 R1 engine, showing the polished, rectangular web crank with lightened crank pins. For racing, all three main bearings were identical with separate thrusts; although this was not standardized by Jowett, it is quite common today. (Woods Visual Imaging)

process resulted in sulphur being present, and the resultant iron sulphide inclusions could have been the start of a fatigue fracture if in the wrong place. This problem may explain why crank failure was not unknown in other makes of car at that time; however, it does not explain the unacceptable incidence of failures experienced by Javelins and Jupiters in the early fifties.

During the 1952 Le Mans race not only did two out of the three Jupiters break their cranks, rather publicly, but cranks broke in race practice, too. Breakages occurred on the Mulsanne straight

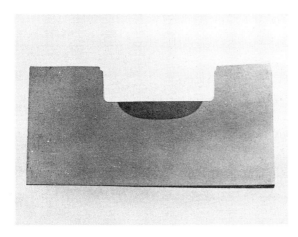

Section through a Javelin crank-pin journal, showing hardening zone kept away from the webs. (Keighley Laboratories)

when pulling around 4,200 to 4,400rpm. This led to the theory that there was a killer engine speed that had to be avoided: for its last eight hours the remaining Jupiter was told not to exceed 4,000rpm, which partly explains its low overall average speed for the race. However, the raised cr may have been as much to blame as the supposed killer rpm.

Something clearly had to be done. On test a crank broke after only fifty hours at 4,200rpm. The fracture was almost always across the front flying web, that is, the unsupported web between crankpins of cylinders one and two; in rare cases it was the rear flying web that failed.

Ron Love of MIRA was consulted. He advised on manufacturing methods: keep the hardening zone well away from the crankpin fillet, or else harden right round into the web. Keep the fillet well rounded. Avoid the need for straightening the crank after hardening. Following this consultation, Grandfield introduced several manufacturing modifications to the crank that generally eased the problem for road cars.

Dr Ker Wilson, a crankshaft stress expert at de Havilland, carried out his own conventional analysis on the Jowett crankshaft. His company manufactured 2,000bhp horizontal marine engines. He also showed that the crank should not fail, but his explanation was that, in addition to the deflections suggested by his analysis, there must also be a longitudinal oscillation, by chance at the same frequency as the rotational oscillation, such that the two effects would be additive. He did not prove there was such an oscillation, he merely concluded that to explain crank failure there must be.

Head Gasket Failures

Another, unrelated, engine problem was head gasket failure. Hadley blew a gasket in the 1951 Silverstone Production Sports car race, whilst leading, as did the R1 in the 1951 Le Mans. The long full-throttle ascents in the Alpine Rally took their toll: a Jupiter blew a gasket in the 1951 (on the last day!), whilst a Javelin in the 1952 and a Jupiter in the 1953 also had this failure.

After much investigation and testing of alternative head gaskets, and even head castings, a major cause was found to be due to liner sinkage – the engine had its cast-iron wet liners seated in an aluminium block with a composite material (Hallite) as a thick lower liner seal. This seal is subject to a compressive blow at each firing stroke, and would gradually compress, allowing the liner to sink. The consequent reduced compressive pressure on the head gasket would lead it to fail eventually.

Firstly, a stronger head gasket was made from a copper-asbestos-steel sandwich, rather than copper-asbestos-copper – but initially for Jupiters only. Secondly, the liner bottom seal was changed from Hallite to Klingerit 1000 compressed asbestos with a reinforcing bronze mesh, a significantly harder technology. Normal practice today when these engines are rebuilt is to fit soft copper seals below the liner.

Improved crankshaft manufacturing methods, a stiffer crankcase, together with oiling improvements and steps to reduce the likelihood of head gasket failures, were grouped together in the Series III engine, released from the end of July 1952.

Testing the Series III Engine

The Series III engine was put to extensive test, initially by three Javelins that were run at the MIRA test track at Nuneaton on a former wartime airfield, late in 1952. Jowett laid out the course, marking it with 50-gallon oildrums filled with concrete. The test track was in its infancy, with building equipment, earth moving machinery, site huts and so on. Jowett drivers, timekeepers and service personnel set up camp in three or four caravans of their own, and the plan was to drive the three Javelins for 40,000 miles (65,000km) each at an average speed of 60mph

Snapshot of the MIRA banked test track under construction late in 1952. A Jupiter under test can be seen in the distance. (Duncan Laing)

(100km/h) for as long as it took, night and day, rain or shine. Relief crews came out at weekends. With stops for regular servicing, driver and tyre changes and any necessary maintenance work, it was expected to take about six weeks. Grandfield called this Operation Boomtown on account of the living conditions, amenities and site huts. There was no artificial lighting, so the cars' headlamps were in use during night and fog. Once a Javelin was sent out with no oil in the sump, though fortunately the driver spotted the lack of pressure before any damage was done!

The track used a mix of concrete runways, perimeter road and tarmac link sections, some of which were particularly abrasive, and tyres had a short life. The Bedford three-tonner was sent to scour the land for new tyres, and towards the end the pile of worn cases was higher than the caravans. On one occasion a caravan caught fire, and with the timekeepers otherwise occupied, the drivers speeded up to almost 80mph (130km/h). The test was eventually completed when all three Javelins had done their 40,000 miles, happily with no engine failures; but it is hardly surprisingly that other things had given trouble, including gearboxes, and valuable lessons were learned.

It was then decided to repeat the test with Jupiters. This almost led to a fatality, because at some stage, when the drivers were tired and the track was wet, a Jupiter slid off on a bend and collided with one of the concrete-filled oil drums: it struck the offside front wheel assembly, and the stub axle broke. The raw end dug into the concrete and the car catapulted diagonally, and as it turned over, hurled the driver out through the hood – fortunately onto soft earth, which saved him. The test continued with the remaining two Jupiters, and again on completion no engine failures had occurred. The Series III engine was deemed to be reliable.

Some time in 1953 a revised liner with a rubber O-ring bottom seal was introduced, following racing and rallying practice, although not initially fitted to all production cars. A chamfer was machined on the inside edge of the crankcase facing to take the rubber ring, whilst the liner made a metal contact with the crankcase. Sinkage

Oval web shaft prepared for a reconditioned engine. (Dennis Sparrow)

was now impossible. This worked well, but the liners were not retrofittable without specialist machining of the crankcase. A large number of Series III engines with these liner seals were shipped out to California, suggesting that gasket problems were of some significant concern in the USA.

Donald Bastow had his own theory about crank failure: this was that gas loads should be taken into account in analysing the dynamic forces on a crankshaft. He was able to show that the crank was marginal without suggesting insufficient stiffness of the crankcase or proposing the endwise shuffle. His theory explained the marked relationship between crank life and cr. Although at this point it was only suspected in Javelins, cranks did eventually break in them too. USA Jupiters ran at 8:1 and of course thanks to their road system, ran for longer at near full power and hence high gas loads. The 1950 TT Jupiter ran at 8.75:1 and the 1952 Le Mans cars ran at 9.25:1. Even the surviving R1 from 1952 was found to have a failing crank when crack-detected back at base.

The black-sided forged crank of 1954 seems to be stronger than its predecessors. It has unmachined web sides for maximum section, hardening zones that did not reach into the webs, and also very careful processing, such that straightening after hardening was not required.

The final solution, for which all present-day Javelin and Jupiter people are grateful, was thanks to Ker Wilson. Following on from his investigations, he drew up a redesigned crank where, if there was an endwise shuffle, its frequency would be shifted away from that of the rotational oscillation and the two effects would therefore not coincide. In so doing he produced the design of an inherently much stronger shaft. As an ultimate but important touch, when this design was eventually put into production by Laystall as the famous oval-webbed crank, it was drop-forged, which is the strongest method of manufacture.

Problems with In-House Gearbox Manufacture

A serious set of problems surrounded in-house gearbox manufacture, serious because Javelins and Jupiters were equally affected, and sufficiently serious that some blamed it for the failure of the company. This problem was largely, although not entirely, hidden from the outside world, but undoubtedly a heavy price was exacted, weakening the company's ability to compete.

Henry Meadows Ltd of Wolverhampton had been contracted to supply the gearbox as originally fitted to the Javelin. A long-established engineering firm, Meadows were very good at this type of work and generally produced a satisfactory product. The two (mercifully rare) faults associated with the Meadows box were the weakness of the thrust washers, a problem of design, and an occasional tendency to jump out. The consequence of thrust washer breakage was the loss of two forward ratios; the Tommy Wise/Mike Wilson Jupiter suffered just such a failure on the third day of the 1952 Alpine Rally.

Surviving documentation attests that 'made here' gearbox manufacture was high on the agenda by the middle of 1949 on the grounds of cost. With Javelin and Bradford body manufacture taking place elsewhere, it was the policy to bring to Idle as much of the rest of the manufacturing as possible.

It had been planned to introduce the 'J box', as the Jowett-built gearbox became known, in October 1950 for the Jupiter and the PC model Javelin, with internal dimensional changes to permit stronger thrust washers. The opportunity was

taken to slightly alter the intermediate ratios. The box actually went into full production almost exactly 12 months late, although Jupiters probably had them from the start of their production.

So confident was Bill Mayall (the new works manager) that he couldn't be bothered to visit Meadows to have a look at their procedures. He was, after all, building the Bradford gearbox successfully. Mayall, it seems from all accounts, was an arrogant man, and although in-experienced, was unwilling to learn from others around him. Disliked by many who had to work under him, rightly or wrongly, he has come to fulfil the role of scapegoat for many of the more serious difficulties. Probably because he promised cost savings, he enjoyed the total confidence of Arthur Jopling (an accountant by training) and the rest of the Jowett board.

At the worst possible moment, in April 1951, the high-nickel gear steel EN36 became unavailable thanks to the Korean war: all Mayall's development work, gear cutters and hardening procedures had been on the basis of this alloy. In June, Meadows told Jowett that they were unable to obtain the material for the order they had accepted for the supplying and machining of 2,000 sets of gears. And worse, it was Mayall's intention, seemingly on the advice of Fred Butler, the foreman of the gear cutting shop, to dispense with the final grind to size after hardening of the internal splines of the mainshaft gears. This final grind would require machines that Jowett didn't have, and which, due to the accuracies involved, would have to be operated by skilled machinists, whereas earlier operations required semi-skilled labour. Any scrap at that stage would be the most costly, as all the previous operations would be scrapped, too.

At a meeting called on 10 May 1951 to discuss reports of increased harshness of the Javelin, Grandfield stated that most stemmed from the gearbox, and presumed that Meadows were not giving it the attention they used to, since they were on the last batch. Jowett were supplying certain parts for these boxes on a loan basis, taken from stocks being built up for the commencement of J-box manufacture. Meadows were barely keeping up with Javelin production, and it was

*Recently discovered
display version of the
Meadows gearbox.
(Dennis Sparrow)*

considered hardly practical to send the worst back to Wolverhampton for rectification. Bill Mayall was confident that the J boxes would be 'vastly better'.

Most gearbox manufacturers employed gear shaving followed by hardening, with no subsequent grinding. The gear was quenched during heat treatment on a mandrel, which had to be quickly removed before the two parts froze together. Some distortion was inevitable, and the trick was to employ steel that distorted consistently, and then to find out by experiment just how much to allow: the splines had to be parallel, and a few minutes of angle could be too much. Gear teeth have to be absolutely true to the axis of the shaft on which they run – it was all a question of concentricity. Meadows spent a lot of money getting them true, and Jopling was all for saving money.

Very careful control of the heat treatment process was required. EN36 is an extremely good material in this respect, tolerant of process variations and fairly predictable. But the substitute steels that were introduced due to the nickel shortage, whilst theoretically capable of achieving the results of EN36, were much less predictable in practice, wanting the most precise heat treatment.

Production quantities of gearbox parts, made at Idle, were being accumulated from the early part of 1951, and prototype J boxes were fitted to most Jupiters from the start of production in October 1950. The last Meadows boxes were received at the end of August 1951, the total supplied being about 17,000. At that time, a buoyant Mayall conceded that there would initially be a certain amount of 'slight rattle' from the first 3,000 J boxes, as 'one gear had been machined incorrectly'; this, he declared, would not affect the efficiency or life of the box.

Gear clusters made from the substitute steel were found to be prone to tooth stripping – a fault unknown from Meadows boxes. Due to the dimensional changes during hardening, and also due to inaccurate machining, some parts had to be specially matched to obtain a fit. Special parts were made in order to salvage otherwise unusable parts, a problem that applied to the CC Bradford's gearbox, too.

About 5 per cent of boxes failed at the inspection stage, and about 10 per cent failed on the 10-mile (16km) test that all cars received, with a few actually seizing; there were examples – fortunately rare – of cars flipping over if this happened at speed. Towards the end of 1951 Javelins awaiting

Brands Hatch, 1976. Geoff McAuley (left) and Pete Crosby. Spot the Mk1a! (Ferret Fotographics)

gearboxes began to accumulate around the factory.

Relations between Mayall and Grandfield deteriorated as Mayall began to test his own ideas in a haphazard, secretive manner, ceasing to consult Grandfield, Lunn or Grimley. Grandfield was nothing if not methodical, and his department had solved some quite intricate problems along the way. Mayall, under enormous pressure to get cars out, if by any stretch of the imagination they could be described as saleable, also began to ignore the inspection department's findings, with the result that transmissions were fitted to cars with parts that were outside tolerance. Needless to say this practice soon developed into warranty claims. An emotional Charles Grandfield summed up: 'Mayall … is not amenable to suggestion or advice – Knowall, not Mayall, would be more applicable. The use of a Javelin by Street and Norrington for experimental investigation … is more likely being used for research into varying brands of ale …'.

Moreover, cars supplied to customers began to display transmission faults, the majority jumping out of reverse or first and reverse, but some baulking or sticking. Sometimes a jump out of reverse

bent a selector, which then caused it to refuse to enter first. According to John Baldwin a few customers were even given replacement cars. About 10 per cent of new Javelins were affected during the 6-month warranty period, the fault usually being rectified by the local agent with the assistance of the hard-working and hard-pressed service department. Indeed, the service department became very skilled at sorting out gearboxes that in truth should never have been fitted in the first place. Furthermore, it was not just the Javelin box, for the Bradford CC box was also proving troublesome, especially jumping out. The same solution, pairing gears, was tried.

By the end of 1951, about 2,500 of the first batch of 3,000 J boxes had been completed. Seventeen concession notes had been issued with respect to twelve different gearbox components. Generally this was to allow salvage by making special over- or undersize mating parts, or special adaptors. The actual number of parts involved was usually in the high tens or low hundreds.

In the last week of March 1952, for example, out of the 125 boxes built, no fewer than twenty were rejected at the final inspection stage, and of these, four were rebuilds from previous rejections! A service department list shows that PC Javelins with gearbox trouble were presenting them at between 2,000 and 5,000 miles (3,000 and 8,000km). The factory was still managing to deliver about 110 Javelins weekly throughout this period, but cars awaiting gearboxes, and also unbuilt bodies as delivered, were collecting around the factory.

As late as May 1952 the delivery of new cars was halted for a time while further experiments were carried out on gearbox modifications, and a report written in June indicates that some Javelins were still going to customers with jumping out and baulking. At this time, the service department reported that 150 (home) customers were waiting for gearboxes. People advertising Javelins for sale were naming the fitment of a Meadows gearbox as a selling point. Javelins both built and unbuilt were still accumulating around the factory, but it was not clear at this point whether this was due to lack of gearboxes or lack of sales.

Gradually, though, gearbox problems eased as machining and hardening techniques improved, especially after Horace Grimley became involved, and it was finally conceded that a machine would have to be purchased to enable the sliding gears to be ground after hardening. Grimley was of the opinion that the latest methods of heat treatment were giving 'remarkable consistency of shape', and that when grinding

was used 'to control size, as by Henry Meadows, we would have both good and quiet gearboxes'. When in July equipment for the post-hardening grinding arrived, he was proved right.

The J box was introduced at Javelin serial number 18,000 approximately, and the following table of gearbox warranty claims (British sales only) by car serial number shows a sharp decline after 21,000:

Javelin 19,000 to 19,999: seventy-eight claims
(about nine per week);
20,000 to 20,999: thirty-seven claims;
21,000 to 21,999: eight claims.

The manufacture of the J box was now satisfactory, given good quality control. The CD vehicles were to use a version of it, and all CD testing had been on this basis. But sadly, after Javelin serial number 22,000, fewer than 3,000 cars remained to be built.

At least 26,000 new, serial-numbered Javelin and Jupiter gearboxes were built (Meadows and Jowett) for a car production of 2,000 less than this number. Further, from the reconditioning serial numbers it seems that more than 2,000 boxes were reconditioned by the factory, of which only a tiny proportion were of Meadows' manufacture. Today, half a century later, as with engines, sound workable gearboxes can be had with careful attention during overhaul.

12 The Bitter with the Sweet

No book on Jowett is complete without an analysis of the end of this venerable company. When the end came, it did so abruptly and seemingly without warning: there was no merger and no takeover, and no badge-engineered Jowetts graced British or any other roads. Such an exit demands an explanation. Not surprisingly, and perhaps with some justification, a scapegoat was looked for.

By the early 1950s Jowett cars had been a regular part of the motoring scene for nearly half a century – that is, for almost the entire history of motoring. They may not have been plentiful, but the fact is there had always been Jowetts. When after World War II the Javelin appeared, here was a fast, well handling car that symbolized the end of austerity, and the Jupiter with its spectacular early racing and rally successes reinforced this. Also the Bradford van, unashamedly pre-war in concept, was a popular and reliable workhorse that provided low-cost, affordable motoring for many.

We have seen how each year since 1949 either or both the Javelin and the Jupiter had had major, well publicized sporting successes. Beginning with the Javelin wins at Monte Carlo and Spa, 1950 then brought the first result at Le Mans; 1951 saw the outright win of the Lisbon International Rally by an entirely standard Jupiter; then Le Mans again; Watkins Glen; and several triumphs for the Javelin. Amongst the high profile results for 1952 the Javelin's 'Best Closed Car' in the RAC International Rally must be singled out, whilst 1953 brought Jowett their second outright win of an international rally (the Tulip) by the Dutch pair van Nijevelt and Eschauzier, in a Javelin that had enjoyed no factory support

whatsoever. This serves to underline just what an advanced car the Javelin was in its heyday.

Thus by 1953 the Javelin was still a much talked about and photographed rally winner – and yet 1953 was the year that everything came apart, with a dramatic suddenness that startled and shocked the unprepared motoring public.

Javelin and Bradford production had had a rough ride from the very start, partly due to steel rationing and partly due to Jowett having to rely on Briggs for the bodywork of the two models. Briggs UK was a large and efficient American mass-production pressed-steel company whose chief peacetime output (at about 90 per cent) was Ford products. The emphasis for Briggs was mass production.

As we have seen, in 1947 the merchant bankers Lazard Brothers bought a controlling share of Jowett, and the management team then consisted of George Wansbrough (chairman) and Wilfred Sainsbury (director) from Lazards, Callcott Reilly of course, and the link men Harold Woodhead (joint MD with Reilly) plus company secretary Norman Snell from the pre-war Jowett company. Chief designer was Gerald Palmer. Steve Poole was nearing retirement but still able to contribute technically, while Frank Salter, as technical director, was the highly competent and experienced production engineer who had developed the ingenious Javelin production line.

Financial Crisis

If the key to an adequate steel allocation was exports, then the key to a profitable partnership between Jowett and Briggs was quantity. The first required 75 per cent export sales, the second

Arthur and Mrs Jopling relaxing at a company dance. (Collection Joves)

average sales of around 150 Javelins per week. To start from zero to reach this level of output was an impossible task under the circumstances, and in 1949 Jowett was plunged into a financial crisis that took a year to resolve. When it was over Wansbrough, Callcott Reilly, Salter, Poole and Palmer had gone, and Arthur Jopling had been put in by Lazards as joint managing director with Woodhead.

This may sound like a night of the long knives, but it was not entirely like that. Wansbrough, a man of mild left-wing leanings, was disliked for this in some City quarters; accused perhaps unjustly of insider trading with regard to a share deal, Lazards took the opportunity to send him packing. With Reilly it is debatable whether he jumped or was pushed; he was an ambitious and determined man who had certainly become weary of trying to wring investment cash from an extremely reluctant Lazards. Salter was presumably considered dispensable once the Javelin and Bradford lines were in mature operation. After devoting much of his working life to Jowett, a stunned Steve Poole was kicked out at a

moment's notice. By complete contrast, Palmer had been head-hunted by the Nuffield organization in the same way that he had been head-hunted from them by Jowett some eight years previously. Wansbrough and Palmer remained lifelong friends.

The New Team

Jopling, a big man and a workaholic, quickly become the Jowett strongman, even before Woodhead's retirement less than two years later. Palmer's replacement was Roy Lunn, who came in from Aston Martin, and his immediate task was to produce an imaginative new range of vehicles based on a single chassis, the so-called 'CD' range, which was to include van, utility, pick-up and car. Initially it was to be propelled by a further development of the pre-war twin, from which Lunn coaxed 35bhp (compared with 25bhp in its final CC Bradford van version).

The budget would not run to a new design, so Lunn cleverly converted the CC twin to overhead-inlet-side-exhaust layout, an arrangement that provided very good breathing through the twin carburettors and large inlet valves. The CD's bodywork was designed by Briggs (who had a small design studio) to suit their production methods. Briggs actually preferred working with Jowett, since Jowett wanted a better quality product than the down-market cars that were the Fords of those days.

The pressed-steel frame was made by the Wolverhampton specialist chassis-maker Thompson Motor Pressings, a company that had been a Jowett sub-contractor since 1926. The chassis had a very rigid front structure – similar to that of the Jupiter – to support the steering and front suspension systems in a similar way. The front suspension was made maintenance free by the use of rubber bushes, a development that was soon fed across to the Javelin and Jupiter. The back end was leaf-sprung, but this apparently retrograde move was necessary for simplicity and to accommodate a choice of bodywork providing unimpeded tail-end roominess.

CD development proceeded at breakneck speed, as only it could in a small, highly motivat-ed company such as Jowett. By the end of 1951 the first Briggs-bodied CD van, powered by the developed twin-cylinder engine, was running and beginning an intensive 24-hour-a-day test schedule. Pick-up and car versions were on order, and when they arrived were considered stylisti-cally good. The car had more room than the A40 and Morris Minor, and (it was believed) would sell at £100 above the latter without having to be particularly austere. Despite the gearbox agony, calendar 1951 was the Javelin's best sales year (in the September of that year Javelins were being delivered at the rate of 120 per week) and the Jupiter's best competition season.

On 17 January 1952, Walter O. Briggs Sr, founder of the eponymous company, died at the age of seventy-four in Florida. It was immediate-ly obvious that British Ford would want to buy the Briggs UK factories, and that sooner or later this could spell the end of non-Ford manufactur-ing by Briggs.

More personnel changes at Jowett included the arrival in the summer of 1952 of Donald Bastow to head up development (a change that would

CD van photographed in 1953.
(Woods Visual Imaging)

Donald Bastow

Donald Bastow. (LAT Photographic)

Donald Bastow B.Sc (Eng.), C Eng., F.I.Mech.E., MSAE, MSIA France was born in June 1909 in Bolton-le-Sands, educated at Dulwich College, London, and obtained his degree at University College Faculty of Engineering, London, in 1926. He became a post-graduate pupil with Daimler in Coventry in 1929, then joined Rolls Royce as designer in 1932, where he worked with Sir Henry Royce at West Wittering. Here he became a respected authority on suspension systems and vehicle ride. In 1944 he joined Lagonda and worked as personal assistant to W. O. Bentley, mainly on the chassis of the new (but ultimately stillborn) Lagonda.

In time, Jowett top management became dissatisfied with Grandfield: he appeared to be slow to solve the crankshaft breakages and had been shut out of the gearbox problem, while gasket failure and overheating of both Javelins and Jupiters did occasionally cause embarrassment in overseas markets. The Jupiter had proved complicated to build, and sales did not match some people's expectations, and the rules on steel allocation, one of the reasons for introducing the Jupiter, had been relaxed by 1952. But he ran the experimental department well, and had a loyal and highly competent and motivated workforce. In addition, he had masterminded some very well publicized victories in national and international competition with both Javelin and Jupiter, and his men had progressively updated the Bradford van just enough so that the intended 200-vehicle stop-gap went on to become a 35,000-vehicle best-seller.

Bastow was recruited in the summer of 1952 for the newly created position of chief engineer. The surprise announcement appeared in *The Autocar* whilst the Grandfields were on holiday in the Lake District. Angered, they aborted their holiday and returned to Bradford to find the experimental department had a new boss. Of course, this was not the first instance of insensitive behaviour at the top.

Bastow commenced in September 1952. Methodical, practical and determined, and with an extremely thorough grasp of theory, most outstanding problems were satisfactorily addressed: engine oiling was given its final improvement by a fully immersed oil pump, a stronger crank (the 'black-sided') was developed, although not introduced until August 1954, and an imaginative solution to the head gasket problem was developed (but sadly never implemented) to eliminate differential thermal expansion between crankcase and liner. The innovative Jupiter R4 was overseen to prototype operational stage, and testing and evaluation of an alternative body material to steel and aluminium was put in hand – this was the composite cotton-based resin plastic material produced by Automold Plastics Ltd. It was used on the R4 Jupiter production prototypes for bonnet and boot. Bastow also commenced the design of a six-cylinder dohc engine.

Under this regime there was no room for Charlie Grandfield and, with the help of Bert Hadley, he secured a position at Triumph Motor Cycles effectively replacing Edward Turner before moving on to Hardy Spicer then Borg & Beck. Bastow did not like working for large companies, and preferred firms the size of Jowett; after the cessation of car production in 1954, he turned down an offer from Ford, preferring to join Metalastik and then Coventry Climax. In 1965 he set up his own consultancy business, and later took up writing, producing most notably an excellent book on W. O. Bentley. He died in 1989.

Phil Stephenson in 1975. He styled the Jupiter Mk 2 and the R4, and did much of the detail work on the CDs. (Collection Joves)

lead to the departure of Charles Grandfield the following April, and Reg Korner soon after). Frank Salter had been found to be indispensable, and was brought back, possibly to help set up the CD production lines. Phil Stephenson, a talented young draughtsman, became unofficial stylist under Roy Lunn's patronage and one interesting task for him was the Jupiter Mk2.

The Mk2 came and went in March 1952, with design studies, sketches, construction layouts and a plasticene model. It was to be based on a simplified version of the Eberhorst frame (still seen as a selling point) with lessons learned from the R1 in the form of a stiffening stress panel forming the scuttle. Again, the bodywork was Italian influenced.

The year 1952 witnessed a down-turn in Bradford van and Javelin sales – the former was by now distinctly old-fashioned, and the CD, desperately needed by Jowett dealers world wide, was not yet quite ready to take its place. Javelin sales were being hit by new models appearing from rival motor manufacturers, and because of the car's perceived reputation for unreliability, while exports also fell away badly at the end of 1951 as world trade became more restrictive. Manufacture of the

Plasticine model of the Mk 2. (Woods Visual Imaging)

Another view of the plasticine model of the Mk 2. (Woods Visual Imaging)

Elegant CD pick-up photographed at Bradford's Esholt Hall. Left: a Mk1a Jupiter awaits its turn. (Woods Visual Imaging)

The CD car saw a little service as a runabout. (Collection Joves)

traditional Bradford ceased, to all intents and purposes towards the end of 1952, at a time when there was still some uncertainty over the CD powerplant – the twin engine was proving thirsty, and was operating with a degree of harshness that engineers thought might prove unpopular. These and other problems were eventually overcome by fitting a version of the Javelin engine.

Early in 1953 somewhere between five and nine pre-production CD van and utility bodies were received from Briggs: rolling chassis were waiting and these vehicles were assembled and put under test.

Javelin body production was continuing at Briggs-Doncaster, but alarmingly at a rate greater than Jowett could complete and sell the cars. Briggs slowed the Javelin line as much as it could, but it couldn't be slowed below a certain rate, and the Javelin was now selling below that rate, at about seventy-seven per week.

Ford UK Takeover

It was formally announced in April 1953 that Ford UK was to take over the Briggs British enterprise, and this was confirmed in May. Jopling felt that if the line was stopped it wouldn't be possible to restart it – first, the workforce might have to be laid off, and second, Ford would be handed just the excuse they needed. In what must have been seen as a nightmare by management and workforce alike, relentlessly Briggs transporters kept coming, and consequently a surplus of Javelin bodies began to accumulate around the Jowett works and, as space became used up, elsewhere too. It was said that several disused wool-mills were rented, and that the total number of stored bodies peaked well into three figures, and may even have reached 1,000!

It was characteristic of Jowett that first the possibility, then the reality, of the loss of their body-making capacity to Ford still didn't stop the development team. It immediately started experiments with a new body material, a fibreglass-like composite laminate and resin plastic, with the aim of making car panels in reasonable quantity without the need for a pressed-steel facility. It was also partly with this possibility in mind that Thompson (rather than Briggs) had been chosen as the CD's chassis-maker.

A New Sports Car: the R4

Boldly, a new sports car was conceived, to give Jowett experience in the new material and to maintain some semblance of production continuity through what promised to be a famine time ahead. Initially called the Jupiter 100 (it had to be able to reach 100mph) but later christened the R4, it was built on a shortened version of the CD chassis, which inevitably meant the cart-sprung rear; but then it would be much cheaper than the standard Jupiter, indeed it was believed it could be the cheapest British 100mph car and still turn a profit. It was styled by Phil Stephenson, developing the theme first explored with the Jupiter Mk2. Again the design team went into overdrive, with much unpaid overtime worked and parts drawn up as they were being made. A running all-steel R4 prototype was under test by the middle of 1953, while a part-steel, part-plastic example was ready for the London Motor Show of October that same year. Powered by a 64bhp version of the Javelin/Jupiter engine, one innovative feature of the R4 was an electric cooling fan, and another was the overdrive unit whose ratio was chosen to split third and top, thus effectively providing the car with six forward gears. Oil-cooling was provided by changing the sump from pressed steel to finned cast light alloy. For ease of maintenance the whole front bonnet assembly could be lifted off after releasing some eight or so Dzus aircraft fasteners (although racing experience showed that a few more were needed!). Some of these features may be commonplace today, but they are examples of innovative thinking in the Jowett experimental department.

Bastow could see that the new panel material might be a way ahead for small firms like Jowett, but it had problems of its own to be tackled: flammability, brittleness, paint adherence, how to pull panels off large moulds. But there was light at the end of the tunnel, Bastow believed, given time.

Jopling Calls a Halt

Javelin bodies arriving from Briggs continued to accumulate, unbuilt, to the point where Jopling had no option but to call a halt – and call a halt he did – knowing full well that his decision might in time spell the end of the road for the Javelin, if not for the Jowett company as a car builder. Unsurprisingly Ford was blamed by many, but it was Jopling who took the fateful decision, a decision that led to redundancies at Doncaster, as expected. All these difficulties were still largely hidden from the general public as Javelins continued to be constructed from the stockpile. The sales decline was not helped by a rumour that purchase tax might be reduced at the next Budget, with some potential buyers holding back in anticipation. The standard Jupiter, unaffected by the Briggs situation, continued to attract some customers.

Negotiations with Briggs did not go well. Over a period Jowett paid for the CD tooling in full (at over £250,000 this cannot have been at all easy), whilst Briggs hinted that it might remain true to a valued customer; but then talks broke down on the issue of quantity. The Briggs price both for tooling and production bodies had increased considerably over their original estimate, yet it wanted a larger first-order quantity of CDs than Jowett could or would afford – and there were suggestions that Ford (understandably) would want to extricate Briggs from manufacturing for third parties: Ford said that after two years they might need all the pressed steel-capacity within Briggs, although nothing was said either way about the Doncaster facility. Meanwhile, development of the R4 continued, and at the MIRA testing ground the magic 100mph (160km/h) figure was achieved – just. But by now another player had joined the game: International Harvester.

International Harvester Joins the Fray

International Harvester (IH), who already had plants in Doncaster and Liverpool, were looking for an additional factory to assemble their new light tractor, to supply the burgeoning government-subsidized British farming sector, still in considerable need of modernization. If terms could be agreed, here was a way out for Jopling, for IH wanted not only the premises but much of the machinery and would employ any of the personnel who were not needed by Jowett for whatever Jowett intended to do next.

The time came, around the middle of 1953, when virtually all the Javelin bodies were built and sold. Briggs refused to restart the line at the reduced rate Jopling asked – no surprise here. On 16 September 1953, therefore, Jopling was obliged to give a press conference. It was a sombre occasion. He explained that 'as his company could no longer rely on a supply of bodies for the Javelin, it was turning to other manufacturing interests'.

Confusion Reigns

The Ford Motor Company felt an immediate reply was called for. Here is the text of a letter to the *Bradford Telegraph & Argus* dated 18 September 1953 and published four days later:

Sir,
My attention has been drawn to the report in your paper of yesterday's date, which refers to the difficulty of the supply of motor-car bodies from Briggs Motor Bodies Limited to Jowett Cars Ltd.

From this report, the inference can be drawn that this difficulty has arisen as a result of the acquisition of Briggs Motor Bodies by Ford.

I am afraid that this report is incomplete and misleading. The facts are that the difficulties arose long before the takeover, and Briggs Motor Bodies Ltd have been unable to reach agreement with Jowetts on terms of supply for future production.

Yours faithfully,
M. J. Buckmaster
Public Relations Officer
Ford Motor Company Ltd.
Dagenham

In October, Jowett's company secretary Norman Snell sent letters to 'All Users of Jowett Vehicles', as follows:

You will have seen in the press, reports that there will be a gap in the delivery of complete vehicles from our factory, and that this gap may be of considerable duration … We are pleased to advise you that the availability of spares will be in no way affected during the period of the gap, and that a complete range of spares for all our post-war models will be fully maintained …

The magazine *Motor Sport* (October edition) put the following gloss on the matter:

This unfortunate partial cessation of Javelin production reflects the complexity of modern car construction … the concern making Javelin bodies is now controlled by a far larger motor manufacturer, and thus a firm established as long ago as 1906 is being forced out of the industry, at all events for some considerable time to come. A significant example of industrial monopoly. Other small concerns beware!

Jopling's original announcement came before October's London Motor Show, yet all the publicity material for the press had gone out and it duly appeared at show time. This led many to believe that the cessation of manufacture was only temporary, particularly with the Jupiter Mk1a on display and still available. Furthermore, the Jupiter R4 was not only present at the show, but had its own roped-off plinth, and another example was available outside for test drives, while a glossy and detailed brochure had been produced – one can only wonder what prospective purchasers were told about delivery times. To add to the confusion there were also two Javelins on the stand, although no CD. The R4 was presented as an accomplished fact, with prices, colours, options such as overdrive and publicity material. *The Motor* of 21 October 1953 went so far as to print almost four pages on the R4, including a splendid full-page cut-away drawing by Theo Page. The article was subtitled 'Mk1a continued, but completely new 100mph R4 model introduced', and a caption to one of the several photographs read '… it is hoped that pro-

Maurice Gatsonides, the celebrated Dutch rally driver – seen here outside the Stansfield Arms, Apperley Bridge, Yorkshire, about to enjoy a half of mild – was asked his opinion of the R4. (S. Wood)

duction of the well established Javelin will be resumed in due course'. It is interesting to recall that Singer displayed their SMX fibreglass sports car at the same show, but it, too, failed to be put into production.

The Bradford Factory is Sold

Negotiations with Briggs and IH continued in parallel, but the head of steam built up by the R4 project was dissipated as a result of the inevitable departure (under the circumstances) first of Lunn (January 1954) and then of Bastow to pastures new. Eventually IH won the day, and the transfer in ownership of the Bradford factory (but not the company) formally took place on 25 October 1954.

The manufacture of spares and the completion of the very last standard Jupiter continued at the old factory until new premises were obtained and fitted out. These were acquired at Howden Clough on the outskirts of Bradford from January 1955, with the move completed by the following August. The decision had been taken that a reliable supply of spares for the post-war models would be assured for a further eight years by the manufacture of some parts and the outsourcing of others, with Briggs supplying Javelin and Bradford body panels

as required. A full crash repair facility was also established at Howden Clough. However, the manufacture of new cars here, even of the R4, was never a possibility.

When not manufacturing Jowett spares, the 100,000sq ft former woollen mill was kept busy with aircraft component manufacture for the Blackburn & General Aircraft Company, and when Blackburn took over Jowett Cars Ltd towards the end of 1955, the oval web crankshaft could at last be tooled up for and put into manufacture. In 1958 the company name was changed to Jowett Engineering Ltd to reflect its new status in the scheme of things. Jopling stayed on as managing director, but by that time his main job was as deputy chairman of Blackburn, which in 1960 became part of the Hawker Siddeley Group, later British Aerospace. Jowett Engineering Ltd ceased trading on 31 December 1963, and cleared out its remaining stock of spares, much of which went to New Zealand where there was a sizeable number of Jowetts in daily use – and in fact there still is! For a while, Hawker Siddeley retained ownership of the names 'Jowett Cars Ltd' and 'Jowett Engineering Ltd'; the company name 'Jowett Cars Ltd' is currently retained by the Jowett Car Club.

Whilst in business, Jowett Engineering continued to operate some of the CDs, including the

Final Financial Affairs

The merchant bankers Lazard Brothers, through their Cushion Trust, bought their controlling interest in Jowett Cars Ltd in 1947 from Charles Clore. Clore had bought them a couple of years earlier from the Jowett brothers via their Snowdon Trust. After only two years 'Santa Clore', as he had been too hastily named, became disenchanted with the automobile industry, and decided instead to concentrate on building up his Norvic shoe manufacturing and retailing business.

Lazard added their people to the Jowett board, one of whom, Arthur Jopling, became managing director. The merchant bankers displayed a marked reluctance to invest any substantial amount of money in a business that needed quite the opposite approach to financing, and had Jowett not been owned by a bank they might have been free to seek investment from whomsoever they could. Sadly this was not to be. Jowett had to be self-financing, or wither on the vine.

In 1951, Jowett Cars Ltd four-shilling ordinary shares were valued at almost their face value. When Javelin and Bradford assembly ramped down in 1953, the factory switched to manufacturing aircraft parts for the Blackburn & General Aircraft Co, another Lazard company of which Jopling was also a director. When the Jowett factory was sold to International Harvester in 1954, cash from the sale was used to pay off all shareholders at the face value (four-shillings) for every share. At the same time, the shareholders were issued with a one (old) penny share for each fur-shilling share they had held. These shares in Jowett continued to be traded, and rose steadily in value until September 1955 when Jowett Cars Ltd was merged into Blackburn Aircraft, at which point the penny shares had reached 3s 3d (39 old pence). This seems to imply that the valuation of JCL had increased by nearly fortyfold in four years! Of course Lazard was the main shareholder and was thus moving its furniture around, but it was a pleasant windfall for those who had held on to their Jowett shares.

It is a reminder that there are shareholders and shareholders. If the managing director of a company has to look after the shareholders of that company, and if most of those shares are owned by another company whose shareholders have to be looked after in their turn, then what happened to Jowett is slightly easier to comprehend. Crucially, then, and contrary to popular folklore, Jowett did not go bankrupt.

Typical 1950s MCC High Speed Trial. Alf Thomas and the R4 at the front of the grid, on the extreme right. Barry Thomas is at the back, on the extreme left, in Alf's open special-bodied Jupiter. Three other Jowetts can be seen. (Ferret Fotographics)

Jupiter R4 in competition. Alf Thomas in the 1955 MCC Land's End Trial. (Ferret Fotographics)

pick-up and one or two utilities, to transport workers to and from Howden Clough. Some vans and utilities were sold to New Zealand. The CD car had its uses, but when Jowett Engineering ceased trading it was pushed into a ravine where it rested, quietly decaying, for a decade or more. Only the cab of the pick-up remains, though one utility survives to this day in the UK, and there are several in New Zealand.

The prototype R4 was sold to Alf Thomas, the Bedford-based motor-sporting motor dealer, and it had an interesting competition history, appearing for the first time on Whit Monday, 7 June 1954. The circuit was at RAF Davidstow Moor in Cornwall, the highest operational airfield in the UK at the time and one of the most rain-swept. At this meeting Alf qualified the R4 in his heat (over ten laps in streaming rain) behind a Connaught, a Cooper MG, a Tojeiro MG and the Bailey special; a Porsche and a Lotus MG also ran but did not qualify. In the twenty-lap final the R4 showed what it might have become – it was the first true road car home, behind a Connaught, a Cooper-Connaught, and three MG-engined specials, but this time ahead of the Bailey special, the Keift and several standard MGs. Alf went on to hill-climb the little car at Prescott, and raced it

on numerous occasions at Silverstone and occasionally at Mallory Park.

Eric Turner, Blackburn Aircraft's chairman, took a shine to the R4 and arranged for the Motor Show stand car to be put into running order: it was registered for him on 2 July 1956. Turner, alas, was a big man, being particularly long in the leg, so after the best part of a year it was put up for sale and was snapped up by none other than Alf Thomas.

Probably the final fling for the Jupiter R4 in motor sport came at the Silverstone Six-hour Relay Race of 16 August 1958. Alf by then had obtained not only the second example from Eric Turner, but also a third in dismantled form that his garage assembled or perhaps reassembled. These three R4s raced as a relay team that actually shared the lead in the early stages; but further into the race first one, and then a second, was damaged. As a consequence Alf withdrew from racing, and after a year or two all the R4s were sold. The new owner repaired the two damaged cars, and one by one they changed hands again. Subsequently the R4 built up from component form was written off; thankfully the other two examples of the final Jowett design survive to the present.

13   Buyer's Guide

Because the engines, suspension and various other mechanical items of the Javelin and the Jupiter are identical, much of the following information is relevant to both models. A section at the end of the chapter gives additional detail that is uniquely appropriate to the Jupiter.

The Javelin, as we have seen, was generally available from 1947 to 1953–54, and chassis number information (see Chapters 3 and 8) gives guidance to the year of manufacture. The chassis number will be stamped on a brass plate affixed to the bulkhead, and will also appear on the front upper cross-member (close to the bonnet-securing bayonet) and, if original, on the top edge of the right-side front wing. On the Javelin engine, the engine number normally appears on the left-side front crankcase on a raised plinth; from new the engine number was the same as the chassis number. If the chassis number appearing on the brass plate differs from that on the crankcase plinth, then the engine is not the original fitment. From new, a Jupiter engine's plinth would have been stamped with the chassis number as for the Javelin, and again with the chassis number appearing on a stamped plate either on the right-hand under-bonnet fixed splashguard (early Jupiters), or for later cars, on the bulkhead.

Engines whose plinth numbers are replaced with R XXXXX are reconditioned units by Jowett Engineering Ltd, whose job it was to provide servicing and spares from 1954 to 1963. These reconditioned engine numbers were a new series beginning at 1, prefixed R. An RO series engine number will denote the fitting of an oval web crankshaft, discussed elsewhere; these cranks were fitted from about RO 10000, sometimes with the suffix N to denote nitrided oval

web shaft. Very rarely Jowett Engineering supplied an all-new engine denoted by the prefix NO; the equivalent prefixes for a Jupiter engine are JUR and JUN. Examples are RO 17726N and JUR 26063N. An engine reconditioned by a dealer might have an unstamped plinth, or the dealer might have stamped it with the chassis number.

Engines reconditioned by Jowett Engineering also have a (rather hidden) stamped plate on the top of the left-side crankcase towards the rear, showing numerical details of any cylinder bore or crankshaft variations from standard.

Only just over 1000 Javelins were built in 1947 and 1948, and these cars are quite rare today. Remarkably few major changes took place during the seven years of production, and most modifications affecting reliability will have been incorporated by owners during the car's life.

Javelins built before 1950 had a rather 'art-deco'-designed metal dashboard with gauges and minor control switches that are square in shape. The interiors of these early cars are slightly more austere than most later examples, although the interior door panels are adorned with a rather stylish chrome-plated strip. Introduction of a de Luxe or a Standard option in late 1949 gave customers the choice of leather seats, walnut-veneered wooden dashboard, enhanced instrumentation, a picnic tray for attaching to the back of the front seat, and various other minor refinements. Apart from being developed for greater reliability, the engine changed little over the period of production.

Hydraulic tappets can be found on early engines, but are not distinguishable without removal of the tappet covers – the later solid ones

Battery boxes under the rear seat permit inspection of the chassis legs. (Geoff McAuley)

have brass or bronze cups, hydraulic ones do not. These solid versions are much more common, and modern replacements are available.

As discussed elsewhere, quite important changes were made to the front suspension for the 1953 model year. The Metalastik rubber bushes that were utilized in place of greased, metal-bushed joints greatly reduced maintenance requirements, and made for a rather quieter and better ride, although in fairness, the buyer of an earlier car is unlikely to be disappointed by the ride quality. The connoisseur may argue that the earlier system enjoys a little more directness in the steering. Nevertheless, it is not unknown for the later suspension to have been retrofitted to an earlier car.

Body and Chassis Condition

The condition of the semi-unitary body and chassis should be the major purchasing consideration. Cosmetic work to deal with external body rust is no more a problem than on any other classic car, except that in general, new body panels are no longer available. Bolt-on wings, however, make for relatively easy repair, and the thickness of body metal on Jowetts ensures that many good sound

examples still survive. Some chassis corrosion problems can be serious, though, and weakness around the front torsion bar adjusters is probably beyond the scope of many amateur restorers. Holes appearing around the rear of the chassis legs need not be too much of a problem, and reasonable competence with welding equipment can make for a safe and relatively simple repair.

Replacement front and rear outriggers, along with new central jacking point assemblies, can be obtained from the Jowett Car Club spares scheme, and again repair is well within the capabilities of a reasonable welder. With regard to the jacking points, they are best abandoned for this use, as they are required to take the weight of the whole of one side of the car. Many current owners resort to using a stout scissor jack under the back axle or front lower spring arms, thus relieving strain on the centre outrigger. It is wise to examine the lower outer side of the chassis rails, particularly towards the back of the car: again, modest corrosion can be repaired without too much difficulty, but extensive areas of rot should be considered as more serious. Lifting the rear seat will reveal battery box lids at either side: early cars had two six-volt batteries, and the two battery covers prevailed on later twelve-volt single

Clubs and Spares

The Jowett Car Club of the UK (JCC) is the most senior of all one-make car clubs, tracing its roots to the Southern Jowett Car Club (SJCC) that began in 1923.

The Jowett Car Club of Australia was formed in 1957 in response to the rising prices of spares; the club went national from the 1960s. An excellent newsletter entitled *The Javelin* is produced bi-monthly: in addition to social news, it carries information concerning the manufacture in Australia of spares. As with the other clubs, shortages are met and the social side developed with active state and national events staged as well as a keen minority engaging in historic competition.

In 1962 the Jowett Car Club of New Zealand was formed. The membership quickly grew as *Flat Four*, a very useful bi-monthly newsletter, began to be produced. The club is dedicated to all Jowett models. A good range of spares is manufactured, and the club exports many of its lines to the other clubs.

Around 1962 things began to change for the SJCC. With Jowett Engineering set to close, Jowett owners from all over Britain began to join in droves, to find that those running the show were no longer Jowett owners! Jupiter owners were sufficiently incensed to go off and form the Jupiter Owners' Auto Club (JOAC).

Following the SJCC's AGM of 1964, real Jowett owners were voted in and ex-Jowett owners were voted out, and the club became the Jowett Car Club. In 1966 the first national get-together was held: this annual event is usually held over three days at the end of May, and attracts a large number of members and guests. The JCC is organized by geographical area, with local sections and meetings plus an overseas section. A spares operation was formed, and local re-manufacture and trading with the New Zealand and Australian clubs ensures that most requirements can be met for its 600-plus members. The club magazine *The Jowetteer* is published monthly.

Close ties were formed between the JCC (UK) and the JOAC. The latter club issues a quarterly magazine (*Journeys by Jupiter*) with a colour cover. Spares, especially those peculiar to the Jupiter, are offered to members and non-members alike.

The North American Jowett Register (NAJR) was formed in 1976 by Ted Miller, and it sprang out of his tireless search for surviving Jowetts across the USA and Canada. A cache of spares was obtained, supplemented by key items imported from New Zealand and elsewhere. Much of the current Jupiter activity in the USA today is directly due to the NAJR.

There are some independent suppliers of Jowett spares and services. Here Dennis Sparrow, in his London workshop, works on a customer's car. (Chris Bayley)

Club Addresses at the Time of Going to Press

Jowett Car Club (UK): Mary Young, 15 Second Avenue, Chelmsford, Essex, CM1 4ET, UK.
Jupiter Owners' Auto Club: Pat Rutter, Byre Cottage, Hawkesdene Lane, Shaftsbury, Dorset, SP7 8NU, UK.
Jowett Car Club of Australia: Peter Carboon, 95 Valley Road, Park Orchards 3114, Victoria, Australia.
Jowett Car Club of New Zealand: Sid Bradford, 106 Dunn's Avenue, Pines Beach, Kaiapoi 8252, New Zealand.
North American Jowett Register: Ted Miller, Box 387, Santa Paula, California 93061, USA.

Websites:

Current Jowett club addresses – http://www.jowettjupiter.co.uk/clublist.htm
Jowett Car Club (UK) – http://jowett.org/
Jowett Jupiter website – http://www.jowettjupiter.co.uk
Jowett Car Club of New Zealand – http://jowett.faithweb.com/

Bibliography:

Clark, P. and Nankivell, E., *The Complete Jowett History* (Haynes Publishing 1991: ISBN 0 85429 683 2).
Nankivell, E., *The Jowett Jupiter – A Car for Road, Rally and Race* (Penmellyn Publications 2001: ISBN 0 9541144 0 X).
Nankivell, E., *The Jowett Jupiter – The Car that Leaped to Fame* (Batsford 1981: ISBN 0 7134 38355).
Palmer, G., and Balfour, C., *Auto-Architect – The Autobiography of Gerald Palmer* (Magna Press 1998: ISBN 0 9519423 6 0).
Robson, G., *The Monte Carlo Rally* (Batsford: ISBN 0 7134 5984 7).
Stokoe, N., *Images of Motoring – Jowett* (Tempus Publishing 1999: ISBN 0 7524 1723 1).
The Motor Year Books 1950–1951–1952 (Temple Press).

battery cars. These covers will allow inspection of the top rear of the chassis legs, and rot around this point will be rather more difficult to deal with owing to access problems.

Whilst the seat cushion is removed, it is a simple matter to have a look at the rear torsion bar mounting points. Serious rust isn't all that common but is very difficult to deal with, and it should signal a bad buy to all but the most determined of restorers.

Oil leaks from the engine, and particularly the gearbox, tend to keep the front of the chassis well protected – every cloud has a silver lining!

Likely areas of rust on the body include the door bottoms where water has gathered because of blocked drain holes and/or worn window seals. Repair kits can be obtained from the Jowett Car Club, although the fastidious owner who requires an exact replica of the original shape will have to do some additional work with filler or lead loading.

The edges of the wings adjacent to the doors will almost certainly have suffered. Simple repairs can be effected in situ, but the removal of the wing will permit a new section of metal to be 'joddled in', making for a more professional and enduring repair. If the front wings are removed, a glorious mud trap can be found in the area behind and inboard of the headlamp shells. Sacks full of debris can be recovered from here, and although the wing need not necessarily be removed to rectify matters, the better access revealed by so doing will enable the area to be cleaned and rust-proofed more effectively. One should be prepared to drill out some of the front wing securing screws: fifty odd years will have taken its toll of the threads. Replacement screws are available, again, through the Jowett Car Club.

It is worth checking under the front carpets where the scuttle side meets the metal toe board, as a leaking windscreen rubber can give rise to rot at either side of the car; however, this is not too difficult to deal with.

The sills might be worse for wear, but because the Javelin has an integral chassis, they are not as structurally vital as they might be on a more

Corrosion can occur between the boot side panel and the support channel. This one has been repaired. (Geoff McAuley)

modern car; however, replacements are quite cheap and reasonably simple to fit. The metal channels that support the wooden boot floor may have suffered owing to ingress of moisture where they join the inner wing panels. Again, weakness here isn't structurally disastrous – they have to be extensively rotten before the boot floor will give way.

These, then, are the most likely problem areas but, as with any car of this age, rust can appear almost anywhere. Javelins are pretty tough cars with lots of reserve strength in the body/chassis, and tales are told of cars that handled perfectly well with most of the chassis missing! Thankfully, present-day MOT testing denies us the opportunity of proving the truth of that particular reputation!

Mechanical Aspects

Having considered the body/chassis condition, the prospective buyer will now need to take a look at the mechanical aspects. In some respects the Javelin has acquired somewhat of a bad reputation. Tales are told of broken crankshafts, worn

bearings and faulty gearboxes. There were indeed a few problems with early production cars, but Javelins, by the standards of the day, were not especially plagued by unreliability. The Jowett company was traditionally a conscientious manufacturer, and great efforts were expended in the quest to get the Javelin as right as possible. One example of this was the tireless efforts to deal with the problem of broken crankshafts, which should now be a thing of the past. Complex mathematical investigations, followed by a consultation with de Havilland, resulted in the development of the 'oval web' crankshaft (for more on this, see Chapter 11). Many cars on the road today will be fitted with this version of crankshaft, quite simply because most of the earlier shafts will by now be either broken or have been discarded. Jowett Engineering Ltd installed them when reconditioning engines, as soon as they became available. It is worth noting that there were actually two versions of the oval web shaft: the first, made from EN24 steel, was introduced during about 1954–5, and whilst being strong, was for some unaccountable reason unhardened and therefore subject to wear. The Laystall crank soon followed, made from EN19 nitridable steel. When nitrided, the bearing surfaces have a very long life: these cranks can be identified by the 'Laystall' logo within an oval, stamped on a web. It is, of course, the Laystall crank that is the most desirable.

Of course, many cars will have been modified privately, so when choosing, it is wise to establish whether the oval web shaft has been fitted, if necessary by lowering the sump and looking – it is worth the trouble.

Another occasional Jowett malady was a result of liner sinkage. The problem was manifested by head gasket failure, brought about by the cylinder liners being seated on original equipment Hallite-type seals. These compress over time, thus reducing the 'nip' of the head gasket around the liner top faces. Some very late engines had a different shaping to the liner and crankcase, allowing for a metal-to-metal liner seating, sealed by a synthetic rubber O-ring trapped in a machined chamfer. These engines, although quite rare, are sometimes found, but for the earlier versions, soft copper sealing rings that do not compress are available from club sources and are now universally used. So long as the liners have been shimmed to the correct height, there should be no head gasket worries.

Wear on pistons, rings, valves and bearings are the same as any other car and can be detected by the usual signs. It is worth mentioning here that, despite popular myth, horizontally opposed engines do not wear out one side of the pistons owing to gravity!

An oil pressure gauge (fitted to some, but not all models) can indicate the condition of the main bearings. Pressures of 55lb/sq in to 65lb/sq in (hot) at 3,000rpm (45mph/72km/h in top) indicate a good engine, but high pressure is not so vital for these engines as for some other makes of car. Jowetts will survive pressures in the 30s quite comfortably, but will probably display a slight thumping noise, particularly during acceleration. This is caused by excessive movement of the crankshaft within the worn main bearing shells. The noise does not signal impending doom and unless the sound is considered to be unwelcome,

the engine will probably still give many miles of good service.

Big-end rattle, as with any other car, may be detected by testing the engine on light throttle. If particularly noticeable, it may indicate the need for fitting a reground crankshaft and new bearing shells. Oil pressures much below 30lb/sq in will probably indicate a well worn crankshaft, and although the engine should thud along quite reliably, it would be unwise to utilize its full performance for long periods.

With the radiator cap removed and the engine hot, turning over on the starting handle may reveal air bubbling up through the radiator. This will suggest head gasket problems, and may well signal the aforementioned liner sinkage. So long as the engine does not overheat, it can be safely run in this condition, but the radiator will have to be topped up regularly owing to coolant being forced past the pressure cap.

Examination of the dipstick may reveal water contamination of the oil. The odd water droplet can be ignored, but any serious milkiness will lead to excessive bearing and piston ring wear in a very short time. This should not be confused with emulsification found beneath the oil filler cap and in the filler tube, which is usually harmless and indicates that the engine has not enjoyed many recent long journeys.

Surveying the underside of the engine will reveal whether coolant is leaking from either head gasket along the bottom edge. Droplets here might be caused by internal corrosion of the cylinder block(s), a problem with some units. Welded repairs can be effected, although this may be costly and success may not be guaranteed.

Timing-chain rattle is quite common owing to the absence of a tensioner on the Jowett engine. Generally this is no more than an aural problem in most cases. Tappet rattle can also prevail, some engines being quieter than others for no apparent reason. Unlike on most other manufacturers' engines, a Jowett's valve clearances increase as the engine warms up. By inverse logic, gaps can disappear altogether when the engine cools (particularly in winter), making for difficult starting. Some engines will have had the valve clearances reduced for quietness, but will be plagued by cold-starting problems as a result.

Javelin engines can be oil tight, but more often will not be. This need not be considered a serious problem unless leakage is excessive, or is likely to contaminate the engine mounting rubbers or fan belt.

In summary, a good engine will be clean and quiet, but a noisy, dirty one may well have plenty of life left in it. Indeed, slightly worn engines can provide quite sprightly performance. When warm, the car should pull very strongly from low revs (about 15mph/25km/h in top gear) without flat spots or hesitation. The latter can be caused by badly adjusted carburettors, but will more likely be the result of worn butterfly spindles and housings. If this is the case, then the Zenith units will need the attention of a carburettor specialist.

Gearbox Condition

Details of gearbox maladies during the cars' production are given in Chapter 11, but the prospective purchaser will want to be assured that the cogs are performing satisfactorily. It is not uncommon for gearboxes to leak oil slightly, and this need not be of serious concern. Gears should select cleanly, although worn synchromesh (second, third and top gears only) can mean that some sympathy needs to be shown concerning the speed with which the changes are executed. If some gears are difficult to engage, it is likely that adjustment is necessary to the selector rods – not a particularly difficult task. Jumping out of gear however, especially on the overrun, may be due to wear within the box. Despite the horror stories that abound relating to column gearchanges prevalent in the period, the Javelin's version employs an excellent mechanism (probably one of the best ever produced), and is not prone to wear.

It has to be said that Jowett gearboxes are not the most durable feature of the car (they are, after all, a development of a pre-war design), but happily the excellent low-speed traction of the engine alleviates the need for constant gear changing. The cars will comfortably set off in second, and top gear can cope with speeds from 10 to 85mph (16 to 140km/h)! Usable second-hand spares from gearboxes recovered from scrapped Javelins are still common, bearings are still available, and new parts such as layshafts are being produced by the spares schemes operated by the various clubs.

Vibration in the drive train at certain road speeds will almost certainly signal that one of the propshaft Layrub couplings has exceeded its useful life. Reconditioned units are available, as are DIY repair kits. One should be prepared for a little clutch judder in first or reverse, because the low gearing coupled with a torquey engine tends to amplify the effects of any drive-train wear. Reducing the engine revs when setting off will usually nullify the problem.

Most other mechanical parts are tough and durable, although engine overheating will generally warn of the need for a replacement radiator core. It should be noted that if the coolant level is low, the temperature gauge sensor (mounted in the radiator header tank) will be uncovered and will therefore transmit a false reading.

Brakes, Tyres and Steering

Turning now to the braking systems, most pre-1950 cars have hydro-mechanical brakes, that is, brakes hydraulically operated at the front and mechanically operated at the rear. This system employs narrower brake linings than later, fully hydraulic models. The early brakes are quite adequate for gentle running, but for total security the later version is preferable. It is not unknown for early cars to have been retro-fitted with the later front suspension units with the twin leading shoe brakes, a point to watch out for. The handbrake should be excellent: anything less suggests attention will be needed.

If original, the car will normally be shod with 5.25-16in (or 5.50-16in) cross-ply tyres; in fact these do not fully exploit the Javelin's fine road-holding potential in the way that more modern radial-ply tyres do – the fitting of radial tyres transforms the car's behaviour. Some owners use self-modified 15in wheels that bring the car's road-holding well up to today's standards, but which reduce the overall gearing, making motorway driving a tedious experience.

The ride should be comfortable and relatively rattle free, but one shouldn't be alarmed at rather excessive body roll: despite initial impressions, Javelins can corner quite quickly, and Jupiters even more so, in the right hands!

Free play within the Javelin steering is not usually a problem, since virtually everything is adjustable (even track-rod end ball joints on later cars). The exception is the swivel pins (kingpins) and bushes, which are often starved of grease and may need attention. Up-and-down play can be reduced with shims, but side play may mean new bushes, and in bad cases, replacement metal-sprayed pins will have to be fitted.

Other points to look for are common-sense items such as leaking screen rubbers, rumbling wheel bearings and malfunctioning lights – just like any other car.

Indeed, despite the technical innovations in the Javelin's design, it is on the whole a quite simple and straightforward piece of engineering, which should present no fears for a reasonably competent enthusiast.

Jupiter Variations

The Jupiter is well instrumented, but do not be surprised if the oil temperature gauge does not work. This capillary device was intended to fit a pocket in the chassis-mounted oil cooler, now virtually never found. The tachometer is mechanical, and is driven from a gearbox fitted to the back of the Lucas C45 dynamo. The gearbox or even the correct dynamo may be missing.

Because of the manufacturing processes involved in the body and chassis, the Jupiter is a very different animal from the Javelin. This is good news and bad news! Firstly, because the car is very much hand-built, it is somewhat easier to dismantle and repair. Having a completely separate chassis means that the body can be removed completely.

The steel bodyframe is secured to the chassis by six mountings: four main ones in the central section, with two more at the rear. Removal of the body (along with the hinged bonnet and front wing assembly) allows complete access to the chassis – helpfully the wings are attached by brass nuts and bolts. The factory brought out a body-mounting modification to eliminate scuttle shake (details are available from club sources),

The Jupiter has a separate body and chassis, allowing complete access for restoration. (David Burrows)

Jupiter steel bodyframe, shown here during priming following major rebuilding work, is largely hidden from view. It supports doors, windscreen, bonnet and tail. (Tony George)

and if not already fitted, this should be considered. Late 1952 Jupiters onward had this feature as standard.

The panels are matched into sets, and no two cars are quite alike, so swapping panels from one car to another will usually require some fettling. Furthermore, since every external panel except the bodyframe is of aluminium, welded repairs may be beyond the abilities of the amateur mechanic.

In general, the aluminium bodies survive quite well, although electrolytic corrosion can occur where the metal is clad around steel frames, such as the front wing rear edges and some parts of the doors. There are usually a few splits and tears in a well-used example, not to mention previous indifferent repairs. Aluminium is not so easy to work as steel, and some panel-men prefer to make a new part rather than restore an existing severely damaged one. Where possible this should be resisted if the Jupiter still has its original body set, to preserve provenance.

The rear side panels behind the doors may be perforated owing to a build-up of mud from behind. The lower part of the door pillars and the floor section of the steel bodyframe can rot badly, and the steel surround for the windscreens may also be suffering from water ingress. As the windscreen glasses are flat, their replacement presents no particular problem. The four main body mounts should be inspected carefully for signs of collapse. The key thing when inspecting a Jupiter is to decide whether or not the body has to be removed from the chassis.

Unlike on the Javelin, the Jupiter chassis are quite durable except for a few places. Being made from high chrome molybdenum steel, they are extremely rust-resistant, and generally (as distinct from bodyframes) do not trouble later owners in the same way that the frames of conventional chassis-built cars of the period do. There is, however, one weak region: the engine-bearer tube assembly where the tube diameter changes from 3in to 2in via the anchor plate, which is no more

Panel-beating skills come to the fore when restoring a Jupiter. (Julian Parker)

than a reducing ring; the smaller diameter tubing therefore supports most of the engine weight. An owner recalled:

> I had a problem on my way to work one day. Hearing a strange noise from the front I stopped and tried to open the bonnet catches. I couldn't turn either of them, and had to use a large pair of pliers. As the second one came free the chassis front end dropped onto the road ....

Breakage of this joint can occur at anything between 25,000 and 75,000 miles (40,000 and 120,700km) and care should be taken to ensure that any repair is a much stronger job, by building up with weld and adding flitch plates or short pieces of concentric tube. Many cars will already have had this area repaired and strengthened.

Because the front cross-tube supports the front bumper, it too can be in need of repair. Rot can occur in the horizontal tube at the very rear of the chassis owing to water ingress, and in rare cases the mounting point for the Panhard rod might have a defective weld. All these areas are reasonably simple to repair.

Almost all mechanical components are identical to the Javelin, although the steering has some differences, notably the use of a conventional rack-and-pinion system. Ironically, unlike the Javelin type, this is prone to wear, and although adjustable to some degree, may require more extensive attention.

Summary

Between them, the four main Jowett clubs worldwide provide a broad range of necessary spares both new and second-hand, and the supply of mechanical parts is such that owning and running a post-war Jowett presents few, if any, insuperable problems. There is a small number of independent suppliers of parts and services, but it is best to

Alan Fishburn at work on the Swedish near-replica R1. During the restoration of this special-bodied Jupiter it was necessary to make a number of new panels. (Chris Bayley)

join one of the clubs and enquire from there. The classic car magazines are of course helpful for components that are common to other cars of the period, such as Lucas parts.

It is difficult to generalize as to which model is the simpler to restore. The Javelin poses the sort of problems that any unitary construction vehicle can. Repair may be awkward and corrosion can have more serious consequences than on its sporting cousin. Jupiter restoration will tend to be based more on cosmetic considerations because chassis integrity is usually sound, but it may be every bit as challenging for other reasons, with serious work to the aluminium panelling often requiring the attention of a professional.

Most mechanical restoration is identical between the two cars. Access to the engine is marginally better on the Jupiter, but because it's so easy to remove the engine and gearbox from the Javelin, this swings the balance back in favour of the latter. On balance then, it's probably an honourable draw!

Afterword

How one sums up the Javelin and Jupiter story depends on one's standpoint. The industrialist will see the tale of a company necessarily and properly torn from the pre-war roots that supported a parochial family operation, fulfilling a declining niche market by relying on old-fashioned values and preconceptions to sell its products. Jowett was to become, as Lord Montagu of Beaulieu shrewdly observed, 'The clock that lost its contentment'.

Our industrialist will recognize great merit, however, in the vision and determination of the Jowett board, who throughout the perils and uncertainty of wartime had the courage and optimism to plan for the future and to capitalize on the engineering facilities that war work had provided. But he may also detect a lack of clarity and focus on the needs of the car-buying marketplace, the result of which allowed the creation and development of the Javelin and the Jupiter, which in turn would lead the company into treacherous waters. It is now clear that the firm's enthusiasm for the product probably outweighed commercial level-headedness. Jowett Cars Ltd should never have contemplated building a car like the Javelin, even less the Jupiter. The company's long-term future (if indeed it had one) might have been secured had it produced a selection of cheap and economical cars, ironically in the mould of the stillborn CD range of vehicles.

Gerald Palmer was not the man to determine what Jowett's customers wanted, or what the firm needed in the post-war era. In all fairness, he did appreciate that the ideal requirement would be a range of low-cost, rugged utilitarian vehicles. But given a largely free hand, the temptation to let loose his inventiveness was far too strong to resist.

The brilliance of the Javelin's DNA owes its parentage to Palmer's own genes: it was a hereditary thing, he couldn't help himself.

It seems that the excitement surrounding the Javelin's innovation became self-feeding. People within Jowett, from top to bottom, were dragged along by sheer enthusiasm for the product. And despite coming to realize, by the end of the decade, that a different approach would be required for the firm's long-term survival, the top brass still went ahead with producing the deliciously irrelevant Jupiter. Furthermore, Jowett's management structure became ever more complex and ill-defined. Throughout the company's post-war gestation, many good people came and went, but somehow the whole never quite equated to the sum of the parts.

So, the industrialist will recognize the signs and symptoms of an organization doomed. In the fiercely competitive and difficult car-making environment following the war, and despite the most worthy of intentions, Jowett's product-led strategy guided it into an unrecoverable nosedive. Happily, however, humankind does not rely on commercial success alone when judging its forebears; how sad would life be if it did!

So for those of us with hearts that govern heads, let us rejoice in the fact that some car makers of the past were similarly afflicted. Sensibly speaking, Javelins and Jupiters should never have been created, but the glorious fact is that they were, and we are indebted to those poor, misguided, foolish, wonderful people who made it so.

Geoff McAuley

Appendix
The Sporting Calendar

The results listed here cover the years 1949 to 1954. International events are in bold type: positions first to fourth are given. A selection of club events with wins only is in italic. Other events are deemed to be of 'National' category, and normally the first three positions are shown, with others where relevant. This listing does not claim to be exhaustive.

1949

January: **International Monte Carlo Rally**. A Javelin took class first (overall 14), another Javelin class third (22).
Early 1949: *Austrian Touring Club Winter Trial. A Javelin won the 2-litre class.*
June: **International 24-hour Race, Spa, Belgium**. A Javelin won the 2-litre Touring Car class.
June: Rheineck-Walzenhausen Hillclimb, Switzerland. A Javelin won the 1,500cc Touring Car Expert class. Another Javelin was second in the 1,500cc Amateur class.
July: **International Alpine Rally** Auto-strada speed test: Javelin gained class first. No final award.

Synchronizing watches at the start of the 1952 London Rally. (Ferret Fotographics)

1950

February/March: Swiss National Rally de Neige. A Javelin was the overall winner.
April: **International 'Vue des Alpes' Hillclimb**, Switzerland. A Javelin came third in the up to 1,500cc Amateur class.
May: **International Lisbon Rally**. A Javelin finished class second.
June: **International Sierre-Ontana-Crans Hillclimb**, Switzerland. A Javelin won the up to 1,500cc Expert class. Other Javelins came third and fourth in the 1,500cc Amateur class.
June: **International 24-hour Race, Le Mans**. A Jupiter won the 1,500cc class.
July: **International Alpine Rally** Autostrada speed test: a Javelin took class first. Mont Ventoux Hill-climb: a Javelin came class third. No final award.
July: **International 'La Sonnaz' Hillclimb**, Switzerland. Up to 1,500cc Expert class, a Javelin class fourth. Another Javelin third in the 1,500cc Amateur class.

1951

January: **International Monte Carlo Rally**. A Jupiter finished class first (overall 6) with another Jupiter class second (10) and a Javelin class fourth (26).
May: **International Lisbon Rally**. Outright win by a Jupiter.
May: Bremgarten, Switzerland. The race for 1,500cc production sports cars was won by a Jupiter.
May: Morecambe National Rally (UK- 2 days). A Jupiter (hood closed) gained first in the up to 3-litre class for closed production cars, also winning the Best Closed Production Car award.
June: Rheineck-Walzenhausen Hillclimb, Switzerland. A Jupiter took class first.
June: **International 24-hour race, Le Mans**. A Jupiter won the 1,500cc class.
June: **International RAC Rally**. (UK) Rest & Be Thankful Hillclimb Test 1,500cc open class, a Jupiter came third; 1,500cc closed class, Javelins took first five places and 7, 9, 10. Blackpool Driving Test 1,500cc open class, a Jupiter came first; 1,500cc closed class, Javelins first and third. Final class positions: Javelins 2, 4, 5; Jupiters 4, 5.
June: SCCA Burke Mountain Hillclimb, USA. Class win by a Jupiter.
July: **International Alpine Rally** Autostrada speed test. Jupiter class first. Falzarego Hillclimb, a Jupiter class first. No final award.
July: Thompson Speedway (USA) SCCA National Meet. The race for 1,500cc production sports cars was won by a Jupiter.
August: *Rallye de l'Iseran (France - 2 days). Outright win by a Jupiter.*
September: **Queen Catharine Montour Cup** Watkins Glen (USA). Race for 1,500cc sports cars was won by a Jupiter type R1.
September: **International RAC Tourist Trophy**. Dundrod, Northern Ireland. Race for prod-uction sports cars: Jupiters class first (overall 18) and second (19) after nearly four hours' racing.
Winter 1951: Stockholm Winter Trial. Outright win by a Javelin.
December: Torrey Pines (USA) day of races. A Jupiter second in a race for Stock 1,500cc sports cars.

1952

January: **International Monte Carlo Rally**. A FHC Jupiter class second (overall 5).
March: Palm Springs Road Races (USA). A Jupiter third in a 10-lap race for 1,500cc sports cars.
March: Vero Beach (USA). A Jupiter third in a 1-hour race for 1,500cc sports cars.

Becquart's Javelin at the finish of the 1953 International Tulip Rally. (Becquart)

1952 *continued*

April: **International RAC Rally**. (UK). A Jupiter class first in Castle Combe test; a Javelin class first, Jupiters class second and third in the Eppynt and Rest & Be Thankful tests. A Javelin Best Closed Car of the Rally. A Javelin crew won the Ladies' Cup.

April: **International Tulip Rally**. Javelin class second (overall 20), another Javelin class fourth (26).

May: **International Lisbon Rally**. A Javelin crew won the Ladies' Cup.

May: BRDC-Daily Express Production Sports Car Race, Silverstone (UK). Held over 16 laps, 37 minutes. A Jupiter finished third in class, the first production car in its class to finish.

May: **International British Empire Trophy** (Isle of Man, UK). Race for production sports cars. A Jupiter gained class third (overall 7) after almost three hours racing, the first production car in its class to finish.

May: Prescott National Hillclimb (UK). A Jupiter took class fourth.

June: **Prix de Monte Carlo International Sports Car Race** (Monaco). Jupiter type R1 came fourth in class after over two hours of racing.

June: **International 24-hour Race, Le Mans**. A Jupiter type R1 took the 1,500cc class.

June: *Margate Club Rally (UK - 3 days). A Jupiter took class first.*

July: *News Chronicle* National Fuel Economy Run. Held over 828 miles, a Javelin finished Best Car Overall at 67.8mpg.

July: Scottish National Rally. A Javelin finished class second.

August: Lake Tahoe Rally (USA). Outright win by a Jupiter.

August: Six-hour Relay Race, Silverstone (UK). Two teams had a Jupiter each: the Sporting Owner Driver's Club finished fourth, the St Moritz Tobogganing Club finished fifth.

1952 *continued*

September: *London Rally (UK - 2 days). Best Mixed Crew award to Mr & Mrs Leavens (Javelin).*
September: **International Stockholm Races** (Sweden). Race for 1,500cc sports cars. Fourth place was gained by the Swedish-built near-replica Jupiter R1.
October: Turner AFB (USA). Stock 1,500cc sports car race was won by a Jupiter.
December: Torrey Pines (USA) day of races. A Jupiter took first in a race for Stock 1,500cc sports cars.

1953

January: **International Monte Carlo Rally**. A FHC Jupiter class fourth (overall 36).
March: **International RAC Rally**. (UK). A Javelin class first, Castle Coombe test. Final results: Javelins class first and third.
April: **International Tulip Rally**. Outright win by a Javelin. Javelins finished 1-2-3 in class and were awarded the One-Make Team Prize. A Jupiter was fourth in the class for all open cars.
May: **International Trophy**, Silverstone, UK. In the race for production touring cars, a Javelin was placed class second.
May: Phoenix Arizona Weekend of Races. In the Governor's Cup, 1,500cc class, Jupiters took first and second.
May: *Ilfracombe Rally (UK - 2 days). A Javelin was awarded Best Performance by a Closed Car.*
June: **Scottish International Rally**. A FHC Jupiter came class second in the Rest & Be Thankful test. No final award.
August: Sheepshead Trophy Race (USA - 10 laps). The race for stock 1,500cc sports cars was won by a Jupiter.
September: *Lakeland Rally (UK - 2 days). Class win by a Jupiter.*
September: *Clacton Rally (UK - 2 days). The Touring Car 2-litre class was won by a Javelin, while the Sports Car 2-litre class was won by a Jupiter. The Jupiter was in a team of three cars that took the Team Award.*
November: March AFB Riverside, California, USA. In three races, in their class, three Jupiters between them posted one win, two seconds, two thirds and a fifth.
November: MCC-*Daily Express* National Rally (UK- 4 days). A Jupiter running closed was placed third (overall 8) in the 1,500cc closed car class, while the best Javelin finished class eleventh (20). Another Jupiter class-won the rally's Concours d'Élegance

1954

March: **International RAC Rally**. (UK). A Javelin finished class first (overall 37).
March: *Intervarsity Speed Trial (UK). In the 1,500cc closed-car class, a Javelin and a Jupiter came first and third respectively.*
May: **International Trophy**. Silverstone, UK. In the race for production touring cars, Javelins came class second (overall 14) and third (15).
June: Davidstow Day of Races (UK). In the up to 1,500cc sports cars final (20 laps), a Jupiter R4 was the first road car to finish.
September: *Essex Rally (UK – 2 days). Javelins took first and second in class.*

Index

Abarth 50
Abbott of Farnham (coachbuilder) 79, 80
AC Cars 12, 113
Action Automoblile, l' 90, 92
Adams & Robinson (coachbuilder) 74, 81
Ainsworth, Harry 95
Aintree 76
Alfa Romeo 121
Alfin brake drums 86
Allard 42, 86, 94, 98, 100, 122
Allen, Mel 128
Alpine Rally 106, 138, 166, 167
Alvis 54
American Motors 112, 113
Angell Motors, Pasadena 72, 131, 132
Angelvin, Dr & Mrs 100
Armstrong, J J, of Carlisle (coachbuilder) 73, 81, 82
Ashfield, Mrs 97
Aston Martin 12, 43, 51, 58, 70, 86, 98, 105, 112, 113
Audi 121
Austin 46, 53, 79, 95, 121, 144
Austin Healey 104
Austrian Touring Club Winter Trial 166
Auto Union 50, 51
Autocar, The 12, 26, 30–32, 45, 67, 116, 120, 145
Automobile Club de l'Ouest 84, 101
Automobile Engineer 12
Automobile Racing Club of America 122
Autosport 67

Baldwin, John 18, 26, 140
Bas, Fabricas 90
Bastow, Donald 137, 144, 145, 149, 151
Baxter, Raymond 89, 90, 92, 93
Becquart, Marcel 74, 77, 81, 91, 93, 95–99, 101-104, 113–115, 117; 118, 168
Behel, Bill 131
Behra, Jean 87–89
Bentley (car) 79, 86

Bentley, W O 145
Bergstrom Air Force Base 129
Beutler, Gebruder (coachbuilder) 77
Bibliography 157
Bira, Prince 49
Blackburn & General Aircraft Co. 151, 152
Blackburn, Tom 133, 134
Blumer, Jimmy 112
BMW 43, 44
Boddy, Bill 18
Bradford (city) 8, 12, 15
Bradford (van) 10, 12, 14, 18, 23, 26, 27, 52, 53, 57, 62, 138–140, 142, 143, 148, 151, 152
Bradford CD vehicles 112, 113, 141, 143, 144, 146–151, 153, 165
Bradford Telegraph & Argus 88, 150
Brands Hatch 140
Bremgarten, race 167
Bridgehampton, races 127, 129, 130
Briggs (GB) 17, 18, 23, 24, 26, 52, 53, 58, 113, 120, 142, 144, 148–151
Briggs (US) 18, 142, 144
Bristol (car) 94
British Empire Trophy Race 76, 168
British Motor Corporation 13
Broadbent, Bill 18
Broderick, Don 128
Brooklands 9
Buckley, Dennis 127
Bugatti 13, 53
Burke Mountain Hillclimb 124, 167
Burrows, Dave 130
Butler, Fred 138
Byfield, Hugh 124, 127

Callcott Reilly, Charles 4, 10-14, 23, 32, 48, 112, 142, 143
Carberry, Jack 131
Carlton Coachworks 31
Case Tractors 24

CD Bradford vehicles *see* Bradford CD
Chassis numbering scheme, Jowett 106
Chiron, Louis 91
Chrysler 30
Cisitalia 50
Citroën 23, 44, 121
Clacton Rally 169
Clarke, Geoff 83
Cleary, Pat 8
Clore, Charles 152
Coachcraft of Egham (coachbuilder) 74, 75
Cochrane, William 128
Coffin, Dexter 124
Connaught 153
Connelly, Don 130
Cooper-Connaught 153
Cooper-MG 98, 153
Coquille, Emile 84
Coupe Cibié 92
Cremer, Dennis 32
Crosby, Pete 140
Crosley 122, 128
Cunningham 96, 122

Daimler 26, 79, 145
DB (car) 130
de Havilland 17, 135, 158
Delage 45, 95
Delahaye 54, 91
Deroy special 12–14
Detroit 32
Dixon, Peter 105
DKW 51
DKY 396 (Javelin) 21, 22
DKY 463 (Javelin) 21, 24
DKY 612 (Javelin) 21, 23
Donington 50
Durand, Georges 84

EAK 771 (Javelin) 25, 26, 29
Eberan-Eberhorst, Dr 50, 51, 58, 88, 93, 95, 98, 146
Elkhart Lake 123, 124
Ellison, Bob 43, 77, 89, 90, 92, 97
England, Gordon 32
ERA 43, 49, 50–53, 57, 59, 73, 104
ERA-Javelin 49, 51
Essex Rally 169

FAK 111 (Javelin) 32
FAK 698 (Javelin) 32

Farina (coachbuilder) 56, 73, 74, 77, 81, 95–97, 99, 103, 114
Faroux, Charles (cup) 89, 91, 97
Faroux, Charles (person) 84, 87, 101
Farr, J E, (coachbuilder) 77, 78, 81, 97, 99
Fedden, Sir Roy 57
Ferrari 44, 45, 113, 122
Fiat 88, 124
Fishburn, Alan 164
Flewett (coachbuilder) 79
Floyd Bennett Field 129
Ford 12, 30, 92, 94, 105, 112, 113, 142, 144, 145, 148–150
Foster, Bob 97, 100, 104
Four Cylinder Club of America 128
Frazer Nash 103, 105

Gabo, Naum 14
Gatsonides, Maurice 'Gatso' 41, 97, 101, 104, 105, 116, 117, 151
General Motors 12, 26
George King Ltd 26
George VI, HRH King 25
Ghia Aigle (coachbuilder) 77
Giants Despair Hillclimb 124
GKU 764 (Jupiter) 56, 58
GKW 111 (Jupiter) 42, 58, 63, 85, 87–89, 93, 98
GKY 106 (Jupiter) 84, 89
GKY 107 (Jupiter) 59, 62, 89, 93
GKY 256 (Jupiter) 89, 92
Gomm, Maurice (coachbuilder) 83
Gonzales 87, 96
Goodacre, Charles 95, 96
Goodall, Mortimer Morris 86
Goodwood 74, 134
Gordini (car) 100, 101
Gordini, Aldo 87, 88
Grandfield, Charles
Grasso, Mr 130
Grimley, Horace 9, 14, 21, 43, 52, 56–58, 84, 85, 88, 89, 92, 93, 100, 111, 113, 140, 141
Grosso, Bud 130
Grounds, Frank 77–79, 81, 97, 100, 103, 104
Grounds, Lola 78, 97, 115

Hackney, Hunter 128, 129, 132
Hadley, Bert 49, 57, 86, 93–97, 101, 102, 115, 145
Haigh, Gladney 12
HAK 364 (Jupiter R1) 125
HAK 365 (Jupiter) 95
HAK 366 (Jupiter) 95

HAK 743 (Javelin) 103, 114, 116
Hall, J F 77
Harrison, T C 'Cuth' 41, 43, 49
Hawker Siddely 151, 156
Hay, H S F 86
Head gasket failure 90, 97, 136, 159
Healey Abbott 70
Hill, Claude 113
Hill, Graham 88
Hill, Phil 13
Hillman 53
Hitler 121
HKW 197 (Jupiter) 68, 69, 147
Hoffman Motor Car Company 56, 58, 130
Hoffman, Max 124
Holdsworth, George 99
Homan, O E 117
Hotchkiss 93, 95, 105
Howarth, Cliff 14, 17
Howden Clough 151
HRG 45, 70, 125, 127
Hume, Anthony 43, 45, 46, 49

Idle (Jowett factory) 8, 15, 17, 21, 26, 27, 32, 54,
    114
Ilfracombe Rally 169
Imhoff, Goff 94, 115
International Harvester 15, 24, 149–151
International Trophy, Silverstone 169
Iseran Rally 167
Issigonis, Alec 13, 14

Jackson Jowett 9
Jaguar 70, 95–98, 127
Javelin:
    body and chassis condition 155, 157, 158, 164
    chassis numbering 38, 106, 154
    CKD 32
    de Luxe 31, 39, 40, 108, 112, 113
    design 15–19, 21, 33–40, 52, 120
    drophead 31, 32
    engine numbering 154
    engine, gearbox *see* Jowett
    engine 14, 19, 20, 37, 38, 54 *see also* Series III
    engineering changes 106–111, 134–136
    manufacture of 8, 24, 26, 62, 118, 121, 141, 142,
        152
    prices 40, 112, 118
    production 26, 27, 142, 148–150
    specification & data 38–40, 48, 133
    testing 28, 136, 137, 140

Javelin-Jupiter 54, 56, 64, 65, 124 *see also* Jupiter
Jewett 8
Johansson 99
Johnson, Leslie 43, 49–51, 86, 95, 101, 103
Jopling, Arthur 55, 58, 101, 139, 143, 148–152
Jowett:
    clubs and spares 156, 157
    crankshaft 101, 107, 110, 133–137, 145, 151,
        158
    engine assessment 154, 159, 160
    family 8, 9, 10, 53
    financial affairs 152
    gearbox 109, 112, 113, 114, 118, 138–141,
        160 *see also* Meadows
    London Showroom 26, 29, 61
    pre-war cars 8, 9, 10
    Series III engine 136, 137
Jowett Car Club 26, 151, 156, 157
Jowett Engineering Ltd 151, 153, 154, 158
Jowett Motor manufacturing Co. 8
Jupiter:
    body details 50–52, 62–65, 69
    bodyframe 53, 54, 161, 162
    California-specification 65, 67
    chassis numbering 60, 62, 106, 154
    construction, design 8, 43, 53, 55, 59, 62, 75,
        161–163
    engine 59, 60, 66, 154, 156
    engineering changes 107–111
    hard top 68, 72
    Mk2 146, 147, 149
    prices 70, 118, 129
    prototype 54, 56
    R1 93, 95–97, 100–103, 105, 114, 124, 125, 135,
        137, 146, 168
    R4 72, 112, 113, 145, 146, 149–153
    road testing 58, 61, 67, 132
    rolling chassis 46, 51, 55, 56, 72, 73, 161
    specification and data 66, 67, 71

Keift 153
Keighley Laboratories 134, 135
Kimber, Cecil 12, 13
King & Taylor (coachbuilder) 54, 56, 58
Korner, Reg 4, 10, 12, 14, 17, 51–53, 58, 146
KW (coachbuilder) 76, 77

La Vie Automobile 84
Lago Talbot 86
Lagonda 145
Lake Tahoe Rally 128, 168

Lakeland Rally 169
Lambros, Jim 128
Lancia 18, 44, 73, 121
Land Rover 13
Largeot, Mme 103, 104
Latune, Jean 79, 97, 100, 103, 104
Lawry 90
Laystall crankshaft 138, 158, 159
Lazard Bros 18, 142, 143, 152
Le Mans 1950 42, 52, 58, 84–88, 134, 142, 167
Le Mans 1951 57, 92–97, 136, 142, 167
Le Mans 1952 92, 95–97, 100–103, 135, 137, 168
Le Mans 1953 104
Le Mans 1954 49, 104
Le Mans pre-war 84–86, 95
Lea Francis 124
Leavens, Joyce 94, 104, 119
Lester-MG 98, 124
Levegh 101
Lime Rock 130
Lincoln Zephyr 18
Lisbon Rally 94, 119, 142, 167, 168
Lloyd, Bill 127, 129, 130
London Rally 166, 168
Love, Ron 135
Loyer, Roger 88
Lunn, Roy 112, 113, 140, 143, 146, 151
Lyon-Charbonnières Rally 79

Macklin, Lance 86, 98
Madera Road Races 130
Mallory Park 153
Manley, Frank 128
March Air Force Base 131, 169
Margate Rally 168
Marks, Cal 129, 131, 132
Marshall, John 90–92
Maserati 124
Mason, Walter 97
Matra Simca 88
Mayall, Bill 138–140
Mays, Raymond 49
McAuley, Geoff 140
MCC Daily Express Rally 169
MCC High Speed Trial 152
MCC Lands End Trial 153
Meadows, Henry, Ltd 138, 139, 141
Mecox Trophy 127
Meneres, Clemente 94
Mercedes Benz 13, 101, 103
Metcalf, Digger 100

MG 13, 44, 45, 48–50, 53, 70, 87, 88, 96, 98, 122, 124, 125, 127–131, 134, 153
Miles Aircraft Co 58, 74
Miller, K B 89, 90
Mitchell, Harry 9
Mitchell, Mrs Billy 115
Mitchell, Nancy 94, 119
MNW 444 (Javelin) 41–43
Moffett Naval Airfield 130
Monaco 41, 77, 89–93, 99, 104
Monopole 87
Monte Carlo Rally 1949 41, 42, 57, 70, 142, 166
Monte Carlo Rally 1950 47, 88
Monte Carlo Rally 1951 57, 63, 75, 84, 88–93, 112, 167
Monte Carlo Rally 1952 77, 78, 97, 99, 100, 167
Monte Carlo Rally 1953 81, 103, 104, 119, 169
Monte Carlo Rally 1954 120
Mooney, Bruce 127
Morandi, Franco 28
Morecambe Rally 134, 167
Morgan 70, 115
Morretti 131
Morris 12, 13, 46, 53, 121, 144
Morrisons supermarket 15, 17
Moss, Stirling 13, 96, 98, 100
Motor Industry Research Association 111, 118, 135–137, 149
Motor Show, Amsterdam, Brussels 32, 55, 56, 72
Motor Show, London 32, 46, 51, 72, 73, 75, 118, 149, 150
Motor Show, New York 56, 58, 72
Motor Show, Paris, Turin 72, 73
Motor Show, Switzerland 32, 72, 95
Motor Sport 18, 51, 150
Motor Trend 124
Motor, The 12, 30, 31, 46, 49, 50, 54, 120, 150

Nash Healey 101, 103
National Fuel Economy Run 116, 168
Nelson-Harris 90, 91
Newcastle Evening Chronicle 17
News Chronicle 116
Nijevelt, Count Hugo van 116–118, 142
Nogueira, Joaquim Filipe 94
Norlander, Goran 99, 100
Norman, Bea 94
North, O D 12, 14
Nuffield Group 13, 48, 143

Odell, Les 90–92, 100

Olivers Mount 114
OSCA 100, 101, 122, 131
Oxford Vaporiser 13

Pace, Ashley 128
Palm Springs 127, 167
Palmer, Gerald 4, 11–20, 24, 36, 37, 41, 43, 48, 52,
    58, 111–113, 121, 142, 143, 165
Pebble Beach 129
Perkins diesel 13
Pescarolo, Henri 88
Phillips, George 87
Phoenix, Arizona, Weekend of Races 169
Pitcher, Bill 104
Police headquarters 15
Pomeroy, Laurence 49, 54
Poole, Stephen 10, 134, 142
Porsche 50, 58, 77, 94, 100, 101, 122, 124, 127–131,
    142, 153
Prescott hillclimb 153, 168
Prix de Monte Carlo Race 168

Queen Catharine Montour Cup 123, 124, 126, 167

RAC Rally 79, 113–115, 117, 142, 167, 168, 169
RAC-TT Dundrod 57, 98, 101, 134, 137, 167
RAF Davidstow Moor 153, 169
Rally de Niege 167
Rand, George 124
Read, Herbert 14
Reece, Jackie 115
Reece, Peter 98
Reidel, Pat 129
Reilly, Callcott *see* Callcott Reilly
Renault 90
Renfrew Foundries 20
Rheineck-Walzenhausen Hillclimb 166, 167
Richmond, Joan 13
Riley 13, 46, 48
Riviera Cup 41, 92
Road and Track 123, 132
Robinson, Bill 57, 75, 76, 89–92, 116, 134
Rolls-Royce 20, 57, 79, 145
Rolt, Tony 49
Rootes Group 53
Rosier, Louis 86, 88

Sagacious II 86–88
Sagaponack Trophy 127, 129
Sainsbury, Wilfred 142
Salter, Frank 26, 142, 143

Santa Barbara Rally 128
Savoye, Jacques 87
Scammel 13
Scaron 89
Scheffer, J 90, 117
Scottish National Rally 168, 169
Scott-Jowett motorcycle 8
Seneca Cup 126
Sheepshead Trophy 129, 169
Siata 122, 124, 125, 127, 128, 131
Sierre-Ontana-crans Hillclimb 167
Sigrand, Mme 103, 104
Silverstone 56, 91, 114, 153, 168, 169
Simca 86, 89, 92, 94, 97, 100, 123, 130
Simca-Gordini 44, 87, 96
Singer 46, 86, 122, 129, 131, 151
Six-hour Relay Race, Silverstone 153, 168
Skelly, Bill 98
Small, Newton 125, 127
Smeeton 90
Smith, R 43
Snell, Norman 92
Snetterton 77, 133
Society of Motor Manufacturers and Traders 25, 26
Sommer (coachbuilder) 79, 80
Sonnaz Hillclimb 167
Southern Jowett Car Club 156
Spa 24-hour race 43–45, 49, 57, 70, 142, 166
Sparrow, Dennis 156
Spears, Harry 100
Sports Car Club of America 122, 124
Springfield Works *see* Idle
Stabilimenti Farina *see* Farina
Standard Motors 26, 121
Stephenson, Phill 146
Steyr 18
Stockholm Races 169
Stockholm Winter Trial 167
Studebaker 30, 123
Sunbeam Talbot 100
Swedish near-replica R1 164, 169

Talbot (car) 96, 101
Talbot (engine) 14
Targa Florio 13
Tatra 18
Tew, Maurice 94
Thévenin 90, 97
Thierry, Richard 127
Thoenes, Mr & Mrs 117
Thomas, Alf 152, 153

Thompson Motor Pressings 144, 148
Thompson Speedway 124, 167
Tjaarda, John 18
Tojeiro MG 153
Torrey Pines 125, 127, 128, 167, 169
Touring of Milan (coachbuilder) 74
Trevoux, Jean 91
Trials (pre-war) 9
Trintignant, Maurice 44, 87, 89, 92
Triplex 26, 66
Triumph (car) 105
Triumph (motorcycles) 145
Tulip Rally 116–118, 142, 168, 169
Turner Air Force Base 128, 169
Turner, Eric 153
TVR 7
Tyresoles 92

Van Vort, Jerry 130
Vaughan, Mrs 97, 99
Vauxhall 13, 46
Vero Beach 127, 167
Viall, David 125
Volkswagen 121
Vue des Alpes Hillclimb 167

Wake, Albert 76
Wansbrough, George 13, 32, 142, 143
Watkins Glen 123–126, 142, 167
Watkins, Stanley 14, 17

Weaver, George 124, 126
Websites 157
Weissman, Joseph 131
Werbell, Mitch 127
Weslake, Harry 10
Wharton, Ken 92, 94
Wheater, Tim 83
Whiting, Lawrence 123, 124
Wilkins, Gordon 89–93, 95–98, 101, 102, 104, 116
Willing 90
Willow Springs Hillclimb 131
Wills Rings 100
Wilson, Dr Ker 135, 137
Wilson, Mike 42, 85, 88, 94, 100, 114, 138
Winterbottom, Eric 87
Wisdom, Tom 43–46, 49, 86, 87, 95–98, 101, 103
Wise, Nikki 42, 89
Wise, Tommy 41, 42, 49, 84–86, 88–91, 94, 96–98, 100, 101, 114, 138
Wolseley 13, 46, 48
Woodhead, Harold 142, 143
Worblaufen (coachbuilder) 32
World Wide Import Inc 129, 132
Worledge, Peter 104
Wright, G 129
Wyresoles tyres 92

Yancey, Earle 127
Yorkshire Sports Car Club 42